P9-DEW-353

EDIBLE TWIN CITIES: THE COOKBOOK

EDIBLE TWIN CITIES: THE COOKBOOK

EDITED BY ANGELO GENTILE

PHOTOGRAPHS BY CAROLE TOPALIAN

STERLING EPICURE

New York

STERLING EPICURE
New York

An Imprint of Sterling Publishing
387 Park Avenue South
New York, NY 10016

STERLING EPICURE is a trademark of Sterling Publishing Co., Inc.
The distinctive Sterling logo is a registered trademark of Sterling Publishing Co., Inc.

© 2013 by Edible Communities, Inc.
Photographs by Carole Topalian

All rights reserved. No part of this publication may be reproduced, stored in a retrieval system,
or transmitted, in any form or by any means, electronic, mechanical, photocopying, recording,
or otherwise, without prior written permission from the publisher.

ISBN 978-1-4027-8557-3

Library of Congress Cataloging-in-Publication Data

Edible Twin Cities : the cookbook / edited by Angelo Gentile ;
photographs by Carole Topalian.
     pages cm
  Includes index.
  ISBN 978-1-4027-8557-3 (hardcover)
  1. Cooking, American. 2. Cooking--Minnesota--Minneapolis.
  3. Cooking--Minnesota--Saint Paul. I. Gentile, Angelo, 1955-
  TX715.E246 2013
  641.5973--dc23
          2012021125

Distributed in Canada by Sterling Publishing
c/o Canadian Manda Group, 165 Dufferin Street
Toronto, Ontario, Canada M6K 3H6

For information about custom editions, special sales, and premium and corporate purchases,
please contact Sterling Special Sales at 800-805-5489 or specialsales@sterlingpublishing.com.

Manufactured in China

2 4 6 8 10 9 7 5 3 1

www.sterlingpublishing.com

Contents

FOREWORD   vi

INTRODUCTION   ix

CHAPTER 1
BREAKFAST DISHES   1

CHAPTER 2
LIGHTER FARE   31

CHAPTER 3
SOUPS, SALADS, AND SIDES   55

CHAPTER 4
MAINS   85

CHAPTER 5
DESSERTS AND DRINKS   119

RESOURCES   150

ACKNOWLEDGMENTS
FROM TRACEY RYDER   160
FROM ANGELO GENTILE   161

PROFILE CREDITS   162

INDEX   163

FOREWORD

What you hold in your hand is the fourth in a series of community cookbooks, created by Edible Communities—a network of regional food magazines across the US and Canada.

It's thoroughly cutting edge—gleaned from the kitchens and pantries of the chefs, drink makers, food artisans, home cooks, caterers, farmers, gardeners, and avid eaters who make up today's Minneapolis and St. Paul food communities. But this cookbook is also an old soul—kin to the community cookbooks that have been published by churches, schools, and other collections of like-minded individuals throughout North America for centuries.

Communities crave cookbooks. In fact, they need them. To document and codify food traditions; to remind us of what's in season; to chronicle and celebrate the people in our communities who feed and sustain us. No matter if today's cookbook is organized by urban CSA members or the teachers behind an edible schoolyard project. Or if recipes once gathered on ruled cards are now crowd-sourced on email. The mission remains the same.

This same mission was part inspiration for *Edible Ojai*, the first Edible magazine, launched in 2002. The simple and revolutionary idea—which has now manifested in more than 70 Edible magazines in big cities, little towns, and everywhere in between—was that telling the story behind our food would encourage us all to eat better, restore our landscape, support our neighbors, and generally make food and drink experiences a bigger, richer part of our collective lives.

Beginning with Brooklyn, and following with Seattle, Dallas-Forth Worth, the Twin Cities, and beyond, Edible Communities, the network of local food magazines in distinct culinary regions throughout the United States and Canada, will publish a series of cookbooks that celebrate those areas where Edible magazines exist. In keeping with the pages of local Edible magazines, these cookbooks invite 100 or so people from the various food communities to submit original recipes that tell something about their place and their place in it.

This particular installation is jam-packed with uncommon dishes such as the pumpkin pancakes from the founder and owner of Common Roots Cafe and Catering in Minneapolis; the scones from Rush River Produce, which is just one of many pick-your-own berry farms that dot the rural landscape around the Twin Cities; several tasty treats from members of a quite active community of Twin Cities food bloggers; the pasty from an Iron Range cook that shows Minnesotans strong commitment to keeping ethnic food traditions alive; the Minnesota Harvest Salad with Chicken recipe from the chef at the Hazeltine National Golf Club, which illustrates how the local food movement is taking hold everywhere; delicious black bean burgers from a Twin Cities television host; and, in a state that loves its hunting and fishing, a recipe for venison from a Minneapolis-based food writer and cookbook author.

Wherever you may be, please consider this cookbook inspiration to get to know the people who feed you.

—Tracey Ryder, co-founder, Edible Communities, Inc.; Mark Weber, Publisher, *Edible Twin Cities*

THE MINNEAPOLIS FARMERS MARKET

INTRODUCTION

Those who live in the Twin Cities and environs have long been known as a smart and progressive bunch. Minneapolis frequently is named as one of the most literate cities in the United States. With our miles of bike paths and greenways, we're often cited as the top bike-friendly city in America. Minneapolis–St. Paul ranks first in the country for volunteering. Our area is noted nationally as a gay-friendly place. We are among the top walkable cities in the country, and among the cleanest and greenest.

Makes sense, then, that eating local would be a way of life here, too.

Certainly a key part of our eat-local movement stems from the growing national desire to know where our food comes from.

Another prime reason for our local food commitment, though, is the especially strong bond here that connects rural growers—in Minnesota and nearby western Wisconsin—with urban markets in Minneapolis and St. Paul: wholesalers, food co-ops, restaurants, caterers, chefs, farmers' markets, and individual consumers. The local food movement in our area is flourishing thanks to this solid bond. Examples are everywhere.

Visit the Wedge Community Co-op on Lyndale Avenue in South Minneapolis on any Saturday. The parking lot and bike racks are jammed. Affluent shoppers from nearby Lowry Hill bump carts in the bulk aisle with young hipsters from the neighborhood. The Twin Cities now boasts thirteen food co-ops in fifteen locations.

Or try the bustling St. Paul Farmers' Market, with stalls of colorful fresh veggies, cheese, meats, bedded plants, honey, and more. Established in 1853—that's right, nearly 160 years ago—the St. Paul Farmers' Market is open every Saturday in Lowertown. In addition to the Saturday market, the 145-member St. Paul Growers' Association has twenty-two markets throughout the Twin Cities metro area. Beyond the St. Paul group, the Central Minnesota Vegetable Growers Association, a member-based, nonprofit association with more than two hundred members, hangs out across the river at the Minneapolis Farmers Market. Plus, neighborhood farmers' markets abound and are being added all the time, from the inner cities to the suburbs.

Beyond the food co-ops and farmers' markets, stroll among the sights, sounds, and tempting smells of Eat Street (Nicollet Avenue) in Minneapolis or University Avenue in St. Paul. You'll find flavor-rich ethnic cuisine from new immigrants who go out of their way to make sure their ingredients are locally sourced.

Even make a visit to Target Field, the gorgeous new home of the Minnesota Twins. Several ballpark food vendors offer locally produced fare at home games during the season.

Plus, city dwellers themselves have been actively getting their hands into the soil. Many tend their own small gardens and then proudly post photos on Facebook of their ripe red tomatoes and other bounty. Others get involved in popular community and employee gardens. Still others look forward to digging into their weekly CSA deliveries.

For this book, we wanted to tell the story of local food in the Twin Cities through recipes. To do that successfully, we felt compelled to cast a wide net and seek recipes from a variety of sources. We indeed found a diversity of folks willing to share their favorite dishes: chefs, restaurateurs, caterers, farmers from Minnesota and Wisconsin, cookbook authors, food bloggers, a natural foods educator, a barista, a bartender, a farmers' market manager, and a television talk show host. Beyond all of these new recipes, we did include a few favorite dishes from past issues of *Edible Twin Cities*.

So feel free to dig in anywhere you'd like in this book and create your own feast of local Minnesota food. Cheers!

—Angelo Gentile

CHAPTER 1

BREAKFAST DISHES

We're big on breakfast in Minnesota and big on breads for that matter, too. Maybe it's that Scandinavian work ethic that compels us to rise early and fuel up for the day. Dining out for the day's first meal is a popular sport in the Twin Cities, especially on the weekends, when most places that are open for breakfast—from tiny ham-and-egg diners in east St. Paul to high-end restaurants in Edina serving lavish brunches—are crowded. So readers will be delighted to find, for example, pancake recipes from favorite eateries such as Lucia's and Common Roots. Plus, bread lovers will find some fun recipes to try here, including Scandinavian flatbread, round date bread, and a tasty recipe called Sunday Morning Scones from our friends at Rush River Produce.

BUTTERNUT SQUASH PANCAKES

From Laura Bonicelli, chef and co-owner of Solo by Bonicelli

These pancakes are the culinary equivalent of autumn at Solo by Bonicelli, a fresh-meal delivery service in the Twin Cities. Laura Bonicelli's meals feature local, organic, and seasonal ingredients whenever possible. She says that as soon as she starts seeing squash at Twin Cities–area farmers' markets, this dish gets on her menu. "I always pair [these pancakes] with my Apple Maple Syrup Sauce. It has a touch of brandy and Minnesota maple syrup. The sweet-and-savory combination is fabulous." Breakfast, anyone?

Edible Tip

Bonicelli stresses that grating the onion is important because it distributes the flavor evenly.

4 CUPS COARSELY GRATED BUTTERNUT SQUASH (FROM A 3-POUND SQUASH)
1 LARGE EGG
2 TBSP FINELY GRATED ONION
2 TBSP CANOLA OIL, PLUS MORE FOR FRYING
½ CUP ALL-PURPOSE FLOUR
1 TSP BAKING POWDER
1 TSP SALT
APPLE MAPLE SYRUP SAUCE (PAGE 19) OR MAPLE SYRUP
MINT LEAVES, FOR GARNISH

Serves 4

1 Bring a large pot of water to a boil over high heat. Fill a large bowl with ice cubes and water. Add the grated squash to the boiling water and cook for 1–1½ minutes to soften. Immediately scoop the squash out of the pot with a sieve and add to the ice water. Once the squash is cold, drain on paper towels and place in a medium bowl.

2 In a small bowl, lightly beat the egg. Blend in the grated onion and 2 tablespoons of the canola oil. Add this mixture to the squash. In another small bowl, stir together the flour, baking powder, and salt. Fold into the squash mixture and combine thoroughly.

3 Heat ¼ inch of the canola oil in a medium skillet over medium-high heat until shimmering.

4 Using a ¼-cup measure, drop 3 or 4 dollops of batter into the hot oil, flattening them into pancakes. Cook until brown and set on the bottom, 3–4 minutes. Flip and cook until browned on the second side, 2–3 minutes. (It is important to not brown the pancakes too quickly; they need time to cook through to the center.)

5 Drain on paper towels. Serve warm, topped with Apple Maple Syrup Sauce and garnished with mint leaves if desired.

LION'S TOOTH EGGS

*From Carol J. Butler,
Wisconsin food writer*

Carol J. Butler is a freelance food writer in Superior, Wisconsin, across the bay from Duluth on Lake Superior, a favorite vacation destination for Twin Citians. Dandelion leaves are an ingredient in this recipe, which inspired the name. Why? Butler says the French word for dandelion, *dent de lion*, translates as "lion's tooth," perhaps due to the jagged edges of the greens, or to their sometimes bitter bite. Paired with eggs, however, they give you sublime color and taste as well as the nutrition from one of the most nutrient-dense vegetables on earth. Dandelion greens aren't used frequently by local cooks, yet they're not uncommon. Some places, such as the Wedge Community Co-op in Minneapolis, carry them most of the year as a green (you can substitute spinach, kale, or collard greens). Additionally, they are reportedly popular among some of the new immigrant groups in Minneapolis and St. Paul.

Serve the eggs as a colorful scramble, with toast on the side. For meat eaters, bacon is a natural accompaniment.

1 TBSP OLIVE OIL
2 TBSP CHOPPED ONIONS
6–8 LARGE DANDELION LEAVES (OR 8–12 SMALL), WASHED, SQUEEZED DRY, AND CHOPPED
4 LARGE EGGS, LIGHTLY BEATEN
¼ TSP GARLIC POWDER

SALT
FRESHLY GROUND BLACK PEPPER
2 TBSP DICED FRESH TOMATOES (OPTIONAL)

Serves 2 (easily doubled)

1 Heat the oil in a medium skillet over medium heat. Add the onions and chopped greens. Cook, stirring frequently, until the onions are clear and the greens nicely wilted.

2 Season the eggs with the garlic powder and salt and pepper to taste. Pour the seasoned eggs into the skillet and allow to set around the edges for a few minutes before stirring. Stir well, cooking the eggs, then adjust the seasonings if needed. Remove from the heat and toss in the tomatoes (if using), stirring to warm them slightly.

Edible Tips

If you are new to eating dandelions, the backyard variety is fine as long as they are pesticide-free. Pick your greens before the flowers bloom.

Optional add-ins: At the end of cooking, sprinkle on a handful of feta cheese or Parmesan for a lovely treat. Turn off the heat and cover with a lid to allow the cheese to melt slightly. Try adding sliced mushrooms, particularly baby portobellos, and cook right along with the onions and greens.

DANNY SCHWARTZMAN

Meet local, eat local at his Common Roots Cafe

Danny Schwartzman's first career was as a community organizer. He ran a couple of winning political campaigns and then worked for a few nonprofit organizations. That background shows through in his Common Roots Cafe (which opened in 2007 at Twenty-Sixth and Lyndale Avenue South in Minneapolis), which is part gathering space, part locavore laboratory, and all about good food.

Why a restaurant? "I always had that idea in the back of my head," says Schwartzman, a suburban D.C. native who came to Minnesota to attend Macalester College. "This is a great place to live and an ideal place to run a local food restaurant. There's a range of people who care about food. The co-op community is vibrant. There are lots of local farmers raising high-quality vegetables and meats."

In short, after doing lots of research about the prospects for a restaurant emphasizing organic and locally raised products, Schwartzman found "there are a lot of great reasons to do it. Of course, there were lots of great reasons not to, too."

So far, the good reasons seem to have prevailed in an eatery that succeeds as a community space as well as a destination restaurant. While chain restaurants make a science of driving people out the door as quickly as possible, Schwartzman believes "you want a place where people are." The café welcomes "people on a date, people studying, people coming in for happy hour drinks," Schwartzman says.

"Things change dramatically over the course of the day," Schwartzman says. "Magically, at five thirty, the people who were here for coffee filter out, and people come in for beers." Sometimes, Schwartzman notes, "it's the same person. If they're here studying, they stay on for dinner."

What's Schwartzman's personal favorite on the Common Roots menu? "It changes all the time," he says. On an ongoing basis, he says, "I feel good about the bagels," which are made in the labor-intensive, boiled-then-baked tradition. In addition, the garden specials change every few days and highlight the chef's "great creativity," he says. "When the food is picked right before you're eating it, the flavor is great, and there's a wonderful backstory to it."

Lots of businesses these days toss around words like *green* and *natural*. Common Roots Cafe provides careful documentation. A section on the website called "The Numbers" breaks out the percentage of "Total Good Food" purchased every month, further broken out by categories including local, locally processed, organic, and fair trade certified.

One of those providers of organic produce is Greg Reynolds, of Riverbend Farm. He is impressed with Common Roots' willingness to so publicly measure and publish these statistics. "A lot of people talk the talk but when it comes down to walking the walk I don't think it always happens. It's one thing to say 'we use local where we can.' It's another thing to be willing to measure it."

PUMPKIN PANCAKES

*From Danny Schwartzman,
owner of Common Roots Cafe
and Catering*

The motto of Common Roots Cafe and Catering, Minneapolis, is "Innovative food made from scratch every day." This recipe is a good example. Schwartzman and his staff use ingredients produced by farmers they know. "We create our menu to reflect the best of the month's offerings from local producers," says Schwartzman, "so we get fresh food that doesn't have to be frozen or travel across the country in the back of a semi. For us, *local* means serving food that tastes great, lessens our environmental impact, and keeps money in our community." This recipe proves that pancakes aren't just for breakfast anymore: dense, flavorful, and earthy, they make a delicious light lunch or snack when the weather gets cold, which in the Twin Cities happens a lot.

2 CUPS WHOLE MILK
¾ CUP CANNED PUMPKIN PUREE
½ STICK (4 TBSP) BUTTER, MELTED
2 LARGE EGGS
2½ CUPS ALL-PURPOSE FLOUR
¼ CUP GRANULATED SUGAR
4 TSP BROWN SUGAR
1 TSP GROUND CINNAMON

1 TSP GROUND GINGER
½ TSP SALT
¼ TSP FRESHLY GRATED NUTMEG
⅛ TSP GROUND CLOVES
MAPLE SYRUP OR HONEY FOR
    SERVING

Makes 20–24 small pancakes

1 Beat together the milk, pumpkin, melted butter, and eggs in a batter bowl or 8-cup glass measuring cup.

2 On a large sheet of wax paper, sift together the flour, sugars, cinnamon, ginger, salt, nutmeg, and cloves. Stir the flour mixture into the pumpkin mixture just until all the flour is moistened.

3 Grease a griddle and set it over medium-high heat. Pour scant ¼ cups of batter onto the griddle. When the pancakes are puffed and full of bubbles, flip them over, then cook the second side until golden brown. Transfer the cooked pancakes to a plate and keep warm. Repeat with the remaining batter.

4 Serve with maple syrup.

Edible History

In *A Cook's Tour of Minnesota,* author Ann L. Burckhardt describes her visit to the Forest History Center in Grand Rapids. She learned that the eighty men in a typical lumber camp in about 1900 fortified themselves for a day in the woods by devouring nearly five hundred pancakes plus jars of doughnuts, all washed down with gallons of coffee.

POLENTA BREAKFAST PIZZA

From Laura Bonicelli, chef and co-owner of Solo by Bonicelli

Recipe author Laura Bonicelli says, "My father's family hailed from northern Italy, where polenta comes from and is, possibly, more popular than pasta. My grandmother made polenta for my father every week. She called it 'peasant food' because it was inexpensive, a staple during hard economic times." In making polenta, the typical ratio of liquid to cornmeal is 4:1, but here the ratio is 3:1, making it sturdy enough to become a crust.

Edible Fact

Asiago is an Italian cow's milk cheese with a rich, nutty flavor. When young, Asiago is smooth; slice it for paninis and sandwiches. When aged, it is crumbly; grate it to use in place of Parmigiano-Reggiano or Romano.

FOR THE POLENTA:
OLIVE OIL FOR OILING THE PAN
2 CUPS CHICKEN STOCK, PREFERABLY HOMEMADE
2 CUPS WHOLE MILK
PINCH OF SALT
1 CUP COARSE-GRIND YELLOW CORNMEAL

FOR THE TOPPINGS:
3 TBSP OLIVE OIL
½ YELLOW ONION, THINLY SLICED
1 TSP SUGAR

8 OZ FRESH SHIITAKE MUSHROOMS, STEMS DISCARDED AND CAPS SLICED
12 THIN ASPARAGUS STALKS, ENDS TRIMMED AND CUT INTO 1-INCH PIECES
SALT
FRESHLY GROUND BLACK PEPPER
1 CUP FINELY GRATED ASIAGO CHEESE
3 OZ (2–3 SLICES) PROSCIUTTO, SHREDDED
2 TBSP PINE NUTS

Serves 6

MAKE THE POLENTA:

1 Preheat the oven to 425°F. Grease a 10 x 15-inch or 11 x 16-inch rimmed baking sheet with olive oil.

2 Combine the stock, milk, and salt in a medium saucepan and bring to a boil over medium-high heat. Slowly whisk in the cornmeal, stirring constantly. As the polenta begins to thicken, switch to a wooden spoon. Keep stirring until the polenta is thick and holds it shape, 15–30 minutes.

3 Remove the polenta from the heat and, working quickly, spread it in the prepared baking sheet, making a rectangle ½–¾ inch thick. Bake the polenta until the edges begin to brown, 25–30 minutes.

MEANWHILE, PREPARE THE TOPPINGS:

4 Heat 2 tablespoons of the oil in a medium skillet over medium-high heat. Add the onion and cook until browned and caramelized, 15 minutes or longer. Stir in the sugar and transfer the onion to a bowl. Add the remaining tablespoon of oil to the pan and cook the mushrooms until they start to brown and release moisture. Add the asparagus and cook until crisp-tender, 3–4 minutes. Season with salt and pepper to taste.

5 When the polenta is beginning to brown, remove from the oven and sprinkle with half of the cheese. Top with the onions, mushroom-asparagus mixture, and prosciutto, spreading evenly. Sprinkle with the remaining cheese and the pine nuts. Return to the oven for 2–3 minutes to melt the cheese. Cut into squares and serve hot or at room temperature.

RIVERBEND FARM POLENTA

*From Greg and Mary Reynolds,
Riverbend Farm*

All year, Greg and Mary Reynolds are up early and out on the land, planting, harvesting, and delivering thirty acres of certified organic produce. Their customers include all of the best-known Twin Cities natural food restaurants and co-ops, as well as eighty or more families who have signed up for a box of seasonal produce every week during the growing season. A hearty breakfast is clearly a must. "Our favorite polenta recipe is best eaten for breakfast on a raw, cold day," Greg Reynolds says. "You do have to be a little careful because you can burn your lip or the roof of your mouth if you are in too much of a hurry to eat." That caution gives new meaning to the term "slow food." (Read more about Greg and Mary Reynolds on page 80.)

1 CUP CORNMEAL (FINE OR MEDIUM GRIND)
4 SLICES BACON
3–4 TBSP UNSALTED BUTTER, TO TASTE
SALT
MAPLE SYRUP FOR SERVING

Serves 2

1 Whisk together the cornmeal and 1 cup of cold water in a large bowl.

2 Bring 2 cups of water to a boil in a medium saucepan over medium-high heat. Stir in the cornmeal mixture and return to a boil, stirring frequently. Reduce the heat to bring the mixture to a slow simmer and cook, stirring constantly.

3 When the cornmeal starts to soften and "bloom," start frying some good bacon (Reiders Meats, Fischer's, Pastures A Plenty, or similar bacon). About the time the bacon is done, the cornmeal will be ready.

4 Stir the butter and a pinch of salt into the polenta. Spoon the polenta into 2 bowls, lay 2 strips of bacon across the top of each, and drizzle with maple syrup.

SWEDISH PANCAKES

From Lucia Watson, chef and owner of Lucia's Restaurant, Lucia's Wine Bar, and Lucia to Go

Lucia's restaurants have become culinary landmarks to good honest food served with welcoming hospitality in a charming space near Calhoun Square in Minneapolis. As *Edible Twin Cities* reported in a profile of Watson, she is a third-generation Minnesotan whose love for cooking began with watching her grandmother Lulu cooking over a woodstove at the family cabin on the Canadian border.

This recipe was part of a larger article in a winter issue of *Edible Twin Cities* on holiday traditions. What are Watson's holiday memories? As a child, she remembers her Norwegian side of the family serving Swedish meatballs, she remembers the moaning and groaning on Christmas Eve when the grown-ups brought out the lutefisk that had soaked the night before, and she also remembers the lefse slathered in butter and sugar. They would open presents Christmas Eve and eat her mom's freshly made rosettes.

"Make these [pancakes] for Christmas morning before you open presents," Watson suggests. "My dad used to make them about the size of a silver dollar. I like them with Tim Fischer's delicious bacon, melted hot butter, and a local fine maple syrup! We also like them with wild blueberry preserves or frozen berries from our summer cabin on Rainy Lake." (Read more about Watson on the facing page.)

4 LARGE EGGS
4 CUPS WHOLE MILK
2½ CUPS ALL-PURPOSE FLOUR
1 CUP SUGAR
⅛ TSP SALT

¼ TSP VANILLA EXTRACT
1 STICK (8 TBSP) UNSALTED
  BUTTER, MELTED

Serves 6–8

1 Lightly beat the eggs together with the milk, flour, sugar, salt, and vanilla in a large bowl, gently stirring until completely blended. Stir in the butter. Cover the batter and let it sit overnight in the refrigerator.

2 When ready to cook, lightly grease a griddle and set it over medium-high heat. Ladle the batter out into small circles, about the size of a silver dollar. Cook a few minutes, flip, and cook until done. Keep the cooked pancakes on a warm plate, lightly tented with foil, until ready to serve.

Edible Tip

Serve the pancakes with bacon and maple syrup or blueberries (fresh or frozen).

LUCIA WATSON

In a "present-tense business," local foods pioneer keeps it real

The walls at Lucia's Restaurant in Minneapolis's Uptown neighborhood are bare. This may seem strange since its proprietor, local food legend and chef Lucia Watson, has been featured in dozens of publications and honored with numerous certifications and awards (including three nominations for the prestigious James Beard Award).

But the white space created by the walls is very much by design, and it leaves room for what is really important—the people and the food. It is Watson's intention that customers be greeted by a friendly face and shown to a clean table. She is not one to rest on her laurels. "This business is very much a present-tense business," she explains.

You see that in Watson—who glimpses the chef's weekend special and declares it gorgeous and then waves and greets a customer by name before commenting on a server's new haircut. You can also see it in her staff.

She is connected to a vision—friendliness, simplicity, good food, and good service. In the early years, she was focused mostly on the food. Over the years, her vision has evolved and she thinks like a restaurateur. In line with that mind-set, her business is as much about simple, good hospitality as it is about creative, fresh food. "It's the welcome feeling," she says. "It's the big sense of hospitality through food that I like to think about."

Though Watson's philosophy is very much in the present, for many she is a pioneer. For more than twenty-five years, her name in the Twin Cities has been synonymous with cooking locally, sustainably, and seasonally. Not surprising, considering that since she first made her name as a chef, she's worked to create change and bring awareness. She's gained a following as speaker, teacher, and author, writing two cookbooks, including *Savoring the Seasons of the Northern Heartland* with Minneapolis food journalist and author Beth Dooley. Over the years, her popularity has increased along with the physical footprint of her restaurant: Lucia's opened in 1985 as a thirty-six-seat eatery and expanded to seventy-two seats just two years later. Now it also includes Lucia's Wine Bar and Lucia's to Go. There's even a dog bar outside.

Watson says the term *pioneer* is an interesting indicator of how cooking and eating have changed with recent generations. She says eating locally and with the seasons is not new—rather, it is the way families have cooked and eaten for generations. "I'm going back to what had been done," she says.

Today, Watson serves in more of a mentoring and big-picture sense at the restaurant but wants to ensure that quality and her principles remain at the heart of the day-to-day operations. So, over time, she's created some purchasing guidelines. These help her and the staff to navigate the available choices while balancing customers' desires. She prefers local and organic—looking for some element of caring for the land. "I just want something I can be true to," she says.

That said, it all comes back to cooking and making great food. Watson finds inspiration savoring farmers' market finds in her home kitchen, exploring gastronomic delights at her other home in Brittany, France, and navigating the seasons and the ephemeral nature of each meal. "The truth is that you can't make it again," she says. "I love that we can't tame that."

SCANDINAVIAN FLATBREAD

From Laura French,
Edible Twin Cities *Contributor*

This recipe, from Laura French, actually originated with Marge Corner, who taught English at Moorhead State University in Moorhead (now known as Minnesota State University-Moorhead) for several decades. The flatbread tastes like a really great crispy homemade graham cracker, French reports. People with sufficient Scandinavian DNA can roll out pieces that are paper-thin and perfectly round. French, however, admits, "My flatbread is thicker and turns into strange shapes—but I'm told that it's easier to spread with honey butter." The great flavor comes from the stone-ground whole wheat flour. Consider the Dakota Maid brand, which has been manufactured at a state-owned mill in Grand Forks, North Dakota, since 1922. The mill was established because shipping wheat to the Twin Cities was too expensive for North Dakota farmers, according to French. "Now the flour is available in the Twin Cities. Ironic, no?"

2 CUPS STONE-GROUND WHOLE
   WHEAT FLOUR
2 CUPS UNBLEACHED ALL-PURPOSE
   FLOUR
½ CUP SUGAR
1 TSP SALT

1 TSP BAKING SODA
1 STICK (8 TBSP) UNSALTED
   BUTTER, SOFTENED
2 CUPS BUTTERMILK

Makes 18–20 flatbreads

1 Combine the whole wheat flour, all-purpose flour, sugar, salt, and baking soda in a large bowl. Cut in the butter using a pastry blender or 2 knives used scissor fashion, until the mixture looks like fine crumbs. Stir in the buttermilk 1 cup at a time, beating well until the dough leaves the sides of the bowl and feels very sticky. Form the dough into a ball and let it rest in the bowl, covered with a plate, in the refrigerator, for 2 hours.

2 Once the dough has rested, pull golf ball–size pieces of dough off the ball and roll them out on a well-floured surface. Roll the pieces as thin and round as possible—the size of a small dinner plate (6–8 inches). If the dough is simply too sticky to handle, lightly sprinkle it with more whole wheat flour.

3 Preheat the oven to 200°F.

4 On a heavyweight griddle over medium-high heat, cook a flatbread for 2 minutes, until it begins to lightly bubble like a pancake. Flip it and repeat on the second side.

5 Place the rounds directly on the oven racks and bake until dry and crisp, about 2 hours. Flatbread keeps well for a week in a room-temperature cupboard.

SUNDAY MORNING SCONES

*From Terry and John Cuddy,
owners of Rush River Produce*

Twin Cities residents love to get out in the country for a day and pick their own berries. Pick-your-own berry farms dot the rural landscape around the metro area, and a popular spot is Rush River Produce near Maiden Rock, Wisconsin, just over an hour's drive from the Twin Cities. As *Edible Twin Cities* reported in a past issue, the idyllic setting, located on a hundred-year-old farmstead, includes nine acres of blueberry bushes. Terry and John Cuddy work year-round to prepare for the thousands of visitors they welcome to the farm each summer.

1 CUP UNBLEACHED ALL-PURPOSE
   FLOUR
1 CUP WHOLE WHEAT FLOUR
3 TBSP SUGAR
2 TSP CREAM OF TARTAR
1 TSP GROUND CINNAMON
1 TSP BAKING SODA
1 TSP SALT
3 TBSP BUTTER AT ROOM
   TEMPERATURE
1 LARGE EGG, SLIGHTLY BEATEN

½ CUP BUTTERMILK OR YOGURT
   (OR MILK BLENDED WITH 1 TBSP
   VINEGAR)
1 CUP BLUEBERRIES (FRESH OR
   FROZEN), RASPBERRIES
ADDITIONAL CINNAMON AND
   SUGAR FOR SPRINKLING
   (OPTIONAL)

Makes 12–14 scones

1 Preheat the oven to 400°F. Grease a baking sheet.

2 Combine the all-purpose flour, whole wheat flour, sugar, cream of tartar, cinnamon, baking soda, and salt in a large bowl. Blend together the butter, egg, and buttermilk in a separate medium bowl. Carefully fold the buttermilk mixture into the flour mixture.

3 Fold in the blueberries. Drop by spoonfuls onto the baking sheet. Sprinkle the tops with cinnamon and sugar if desired. Bake until light golden brown, about 25 minutes. Transfer to a wire rack to cool.

CRANBERRY ORANGE DATE BREAD

From Kate Selner, writer of the blog Kate in the Kitchen

Cranberries and oranges make Kate Selner think of her childhood, as her mom made a salad with these two components every Christmas. Her mom would grind the cranberries and oranges fresh, with a hand-cranked grinder clamped to the counter. The smell meant Christmas, Selner says. "I didn't like the salad then, but these two flavors together are one of the best matches I know in baking." Kate's Twin Cities blog focusing on food and life can be found at KateintheKitchen.com.

1 CUP FRESH OR FROZEN
    CRANBERRIES
1 CUP CHOPPED DATES
2 TBSP UNSALTED BUTTER
GRATED ZEST OF 1 ORANGE
½ CUP ORANGE JUICE
2 CUPS ALL-PURPOSE FLOUR
¾ CUP SUGAR

1½ TSP BAKING POWDER
1 TSP BAKING SODA
½ TSP SALT
1 LARGE EGG
1 CUP COARSELY CHOPPED PECANS
    (OPTIONAL)

Makes 1 (9 x 5-inch) loaf

1 Preheat the oven to 325°F. Coat a 9 x 5-inch loaf pan with cooking spray.

2 Combine the cranberries, dates, butter, and 2 tablespoons of water in a medium saucepan. Bring to a low simmer over medium-low heat, stirring occasionally, and cook for about 5 minutes. Some of the berries should start popping, but you want them to retain their shape as much as possible. Turn off the heat and stir in the orange zest and orange juice. Let cool until barely room temperature.

3 Combine the flour, sugar, baking powder, baking soda, and salt in a large bowl. In a small bowl, beat the egg. Add the egg and cranberry mixture to the flour mixture, stirring just until moistened. Fold in the pecans (if using).

4 Spoon the mixture into the prepared loaf pan. Bake until a wooden pick inserted near the center comes out clean, about 1 hour. Cool for 10 minutes in the pan. Turn out onto a wire rack to cool completely.

SWEET CORN AREPAS WITH RED PEPPER AND VEGAN SAUSAGE

From French Meadow Bakery

French Meadow Bakery and Cafe, in the bustling Wedge neighborhood of Minneapolis, is a treasure trove of locally sourced food. Nationally acclaimed for its natural sourdough loaves and whole-grain baked goods, it is home to a sunny, lively café. The meeting place for early business gatherings, lunch dates, after-work drinks, and casual dinners, it serves a menu of globally inspired, locally sourced fare.

This vegan recipe for sweet corn arepas, from Venezuela, substitutes a mix of frozen corn kernels and cornmeal for the traditional arepa flour (precooked cornmeal) and tops the cooked cakes with vegan sausage to create a flavorful and hearty breakfast. If your guests aren't vegan, go ahead and replace the vegan sausage with the real thing, and top each arepa with a fried egg.

Edible Tips

Using corn kernels that are still frozen is essential here because thawed corn and fresh kernels contain too much water.

Balsamic glaze makes a great accompaniment to arepas. You can find balsamic glaze in the vinegar aisle of most supermarkets and grocery stores, or make your own. Bring 1 cup balsamic vinegar to a boil in a small saucepan over high heat. Reduce to a simmer and cook until the liquid is reduced to ⅓ or ¼ cup. Pour into a glass jar.

FOR THE AREPA DOUGH:
8 CUPS FROZEN CORN KERNELS
1 CUP CORNMEAL
1 CUP CHOPPED ONION
1 TBSP GROUND CUMIN
1 TBSP FRESHLY GROUND WHITE PEPPER
2 BUNCHES SCALLIONS, WHITE PARTS ONLY, MINCED
SALT
1 CUP HOT WATER

FOR THE AREPA FILLING:
1 TBSP SUNFLOWER OR OLIVE OIL
12 OZ VEGAN SAUSAGE, CRUMBLED
1 CUP CHOPPED RED BELL PEPPERS

Serves 4–6

MAKE THE AREPA DOUGH:

1 In a food processor, combine the frozen corn kernels, cornmeal, onion, cumin, and white pepper, and process until the corn kernels and onion are minced and incorporated into the cornmeal. Turn into a large bowl, toss in the scallions, and season with salt to taste. Using a fork, toss in about 1 cup hot water, a little at a time, enough to make a soft dough (you may need a little more or a little less water, so stop before the dough gets runny). Let the dough stand about 5 minutes so that the water is fully absorbed by the cornmeal.

MAKE THE FILLING:

2 Heat the oil in a medium skillet over medium heat. Add the sausage and peppers and cook until the peppers are tender and the sausage is cooked through, about 10 minutes.

TO FINISH THE AREPAS:

3 Lightly grease a nonstick skillet or heavy griddle and set it over medium-high heat. Put about ½ cup of arepa dough onto the skillet and flatten slightly with the back of a spatula. Repeat with as much of the dough as the skillet or griddle will accommodate without crowding. Cook until the bottoms are nicely browned, about 5 minutes. Flip and continue cooking until the arepas are heated through, 3–5 minutes. Set arepas aside and cook remaining dough in same manner.

4 Divide sausage-pepper mixture evenly among half of arepas and top each with another arepa. Return stuffed arepas to skillet to cook for another 5 minutes, pressing the top arepa with a spatula.

SWEET PORRIDGE APPLES

From Hannah Barnstable, co-owner of Seven Sundays Everyday Muesli

Autumn is apple time in Minnesota—lots of apples! Just look at the large number and variety of apples that fill Twin Cities–area farmers' markets each week. Hannah Barnstable says she came up with this recipe after "trying to find uses for the buckets of apples I was bringing home every week from the farmers' market." For this recipe, she says she loves "how the rich, sweet porridge is perfectly offset by the tartness of the apples." They are individually portioned, so they are perfect for a brunch or even as a festive dessert served with a scoop of vanilla ice cream.

Edible Artisans

Hannah and Brady Barnstable, owners of Seven Sundays Everyday Muesli in Minneapolis, are committed to sustainability, making their gourmet mueslis with "real food" from local, sustainable farms. Ingredients include three types of whole grains, crunchy nuts, nutrient-packed seeds, and sweet, chewy fruits—no puffs, flakes, shreds, or preservatives here. And the Seven Sundays name? "Sunday is a day for few expectations, feeling relaxed and energized," says Hannah. "Further," she says, "as makers of breakfast food, the Barnstables wanted to encourage that Sunday mentality all week long."

4 MEDIUM-LARGE BAKING APPLES, SUCH AS HARALSONS
½ CUP THICK OR REGULAR (OLD-FASHIONED) ROLLED OATS
2 TBSP UNSWEETENED SHREDDED COCONUT
2 TBSP HULLED PUMPKIN SEEDS (PEPITAS)
2 TBSP HULLED SUNFLOWER SEEDS
¼ CUP DRIED CURRANTS
¼ CUP WALNUTS
1 TBSP GROUND CINNAMON
½ TSP GROUND ALLSPICE
3 TBSP BUTTER
¼ CUP PACKED LIGHT BROWN SUGAR
1 TSP VANILLA EXTRACT
4 TBSP SWEETENED CONDENSED MILK

Serves 4

1 Preheat the oven to 350°F.

2 Cut a thin slice from the bottom of the apples so that they stand upright. Use a melon baller to cut out a 1½-inch-diameter hole in the top of each apple. Scoop out and discard the insides of the fruit, leaving a shell about ½ inch thick. Take care not to cut all the way through the sides or bottom of the apple.

3 Combine the oats, coconut, pumpkin seeds, sunflower seeds, currants, walnuts, cinnamon, and allspice in a medium bowl. Combine the butter, brown sugar, and vanilla in a medium saucepan and cook over very low heat until the butter is melted, whisking frequently. Remove from the heat and stir in the dry ingredients.

4 Fill each apple with 1½ teaspoons water. Divide the filling among the apples, using a small spoon and filling to within ¼ inch of the top of the apple. Drizzle 1 tablespoon condensed milk over the filling in each apple. Sprinkle any remaining filling on top of the condensed milk. Place the apples in a baking dish and bake until bubbling and caramelized, about 20 minutes.

TURNIP RÖSTI

From Kat Nelson,
Edible Twin Cities *contributor*

"Though rösti, a beloved Swiss dish, is traditionally made with potatoes, using turnips in their place adds a pleasing bit of sweet sharpness," says Kat Nelson, the creator of this recipe, which appeared in a past issue of *Edible Twin Cities*. "This rösti is good with poached eggs for breakfast or for a light supper with a simple arugula salad and a generous spoonful of sour cream or crème fraîche."

Edible Fact

For years, turnips have gotten a bad rap as being too strong in flavor and too coarse in texture. The secret is the size: the smaller, the sweeter. When young, this round apple-size root vegetable is mild in flavor and its juicy crispness makes it a nice addition to salads, especially slaws. Nutritionists tout turnips for their cancer-fighting compounds, not to mention their abundant fiber and vitamins.

5 MEDIUM TURNIPS, PEELED AND HALVED
4 SLICES BACON
3 SCALLIONS, CHOPPED
1 CUP GRATED GRUYÈRE, RACLETTE, OR COMTÉ CHEESE
SALT
FRESHLY GROUND BLACK PEPPER
VEGETABLE OIL (OPTIONAL)

Serves 4

1 In a medium saucepan of boiling salted water, cook the turnip halves until just tender but not fully cooked, about 10 minutes. Drain the turnips and let cool.

2 Meanwhile, in a well-seasoned 12-inch cast-iron or nonstick skillet, cook the bacon until crisp, reserving the drippings. Crumble the bacon into a large bowl.

3 Using the large holes on a box grater, grate the turnips and add them to the bowl with the bacon. Add the scallions, cheese, and salt and pepper to taste and mix well.

4 Heat the bacon drippings over medium-high heat. (There should be enough grease to coat the bottom of the skillet; if not, add a little vegetable oil.) Add the turnip mixture to the skillet and pat with the back of a spatula or wooden spoon until it is about ¼ inch thick so you can flip it easily. Cook until browned and crisp on the bottom, 5–10 minutes. Transfer the rösti to a plate; then flip it back into the skillet with the crisp side up. Add oil to the skillet if needed. Cook the other side until it is browned and crisp. Cut into wedges to serve.

APPLE MAPLE SYRUP SAUCE

From Laura Bonicelli, chef and co-owner of Solo by Bonicelli

This is a simple seasonal sauce that pairs with everything from **Laura Bonicelli's** Butternut Squash Pancakes (page 3) to her ice cream. Bonicelli tries to feature local, organic, and seasonal ingredients whenever possible in her menus. The syrup, Bonicelli says, "fills the house with a comforting aroma that is even better than apple pie." She notes that the brandy adds complexity to the flavor but can be omitted.

3 CRISPY, TART APPLES
(PREFERABLY MINNESOTA-
GROWN HARALSONS)

2 TBSP UNSALTED BUTTER

1 CUP MAPLE SYRUP

¼ CUP BRANDY

Serves 4

1 Peel and cut the apples into quarters. Using a melon baller, scoop out the core, and cut each quarter lengthwise into ¼-inch-thick slices.

2 Melt the butter in a medium skillet over medium heat. When the foam subsides, add the apples and cook slowly until softened and browned, about 5 minutes.

3 Add the maple syrup and cook until the combination begins to bubble and is thick enough to coat the back of a spoon.

4 Carefully pour in the brandy and cook for 1–2 minutes to cook off the alcohol. Serve warm with pancakes, pork, or your favorite ice cream. Store leftover sauce in the refrigerator in an airtight container for up to a week.

BLUEBERRY-LEMON OVEN PANCAKE

*From Beth Dooley,
Minneapolis food writer*

Many of Minnesota's pioneers in the early to mid-1800s were German. This is a twist on *pfannkuchen*, a simple German oven pancake that puffs up in the oven to be golden and crusty on the outside and tender within. Food writer Beth Dooley says this is delicious for breakfast drizzled with fresh lemon juice as it comes hot from the oven. Add more fresh berries before serving, if you wish. Get everyone to the table the minute this pancake emerges; it actually deflates the longer it sits.

3 LARGE EGGS
¾ CUP WHOLE MILK
¾ CUP ALL-PURPOSE FLOUR
1 TSP VANILLA EXTRACT
2 TSP GRATED LEMON ZEST
½ STICK (4 TBSP) UNSALTED
　BUTTER, MELTED

1 CUP BLUEBERRIES
1 LEMON, HALVED AND ONE HALF
　THINLY SLICED
2 TBSP CONFECTIONERS' SUGAR

Serves 4

1 Preheat the oven to 400°F.

2 Whisk together the eggs and milk in a medium bowl until blended. Add the flour a little at a time, whisking after each addition until the flour is fully incorporated.

3 Whisk in the vanilla, lemon zest, and 2 tablespoons of the melted butter.

4 Place the remaining 2 tablespoons melted butter in a medium oven-proof skillet, preferably cast-iron. Set the pan over medium-high heat and swirl to coat the bottom and sides of the pan. Remove from the heat and pour the batter into the pan. Scatter the blueberries over the batter.

5 Bake the pancake for 15 minutes. Reduce the oven temperature to 350°F and bake until the pancake is puffy and the edges are golden, 10–15 minutes.

6 Squeeze the juice from a lemon half over the pancake. Using a sieve, sift the confectioners' sugar evenly over the top.

7 Cut the pancake into 4 wedges and serve it right out of the pan. Garnish with the lemon slices.

BLUEBERRY SYRUP

*From Kate Selner, writer of
the blog* Kate in the Kitchen

Blueberry syrup has been one of Kate Selner's favorites since childhood. She came up with this recipe because she wanted something that was flavorful without the corn syrup. "This is the easiest way to make breakfast amazing," she says. Use the syrup on pancakes or waffles. Selner, a Twin Cities blog focusing on food and life, can be found at KateintheKitchen.com.

½ CUP SUGAR
2 TBSP CORNSTARCH
4 CUPS BLUEBERRIES

Makes about 1 quart

1 Combine the sugar and cornstarch in a medium saucepan. Whisk in 1 cup of water.

2 Place the pan over medium heat and add the blueberries. Cook, stirring occasionally, until the mixture comes to a boil. Reduce to a simmer and cook until thickened and the berries have burst, about 10 minutes.

3 Let the syrup cool. Then pour into a quart jar with a tight-fitting lid. The syrup can be kept in the refrigerator for about 2 weeks.

CORNY CORNBREAD

*From Beth Dooley,
Minneapolis food writer*

Hard to believe, but sometime around August we all begin to tire of the fresh corn we've been enjoying from area farms, and so we look for new ways to enjoy its golden plenty. The sweet fresh corn kernels in Beth Dooley's tender cornbread add flavor and texture.

1 CUP MEDIUM-GRIND CORNMEAL
1 CUP ALL-PURPOSE FLOUR
1 TBSP BAKING POWDER
¼ TSP SALT
1 CUP BUTTERMILK
1 LARGE EGG

⅔ STICK (5⅓ TBSP) BUTTER, MELTED
¼ CUP HONEY
1 CUP FRESH CORN KERNELS

Serves 6–8

1 Preheat the oven to 350°F. Lightly grease a 9-inch square baking pan.

2 Sift the cornmeal, flour, baking powder, and salt together into a medium bowl. Stir in the buttermilk, egg, butter, and honey with a wooden spoon until the ingredients are combined. Do not overmix. Fold in the corn kernels.

3 Turn the batter into the prepared pan and bake until a toothpick inserted in the center comes out clean, 20–25 minutes.

4 Let cool in the pan on a wire rack for a few minutes before cutting into squares.

KIDS COOK POTATO AND CARROT RÖSTI CAKES

From Kids Cook

Kids Cook was started in 2005 by Robin and Starla Krause and Susan Teleen, who volunteered to introduce good and tasty food to the children at Loring Community School in north Minneapolis. The program has grown to include the Loring Schoolyard Garden, where kids can plant, tend, and harvest their food as well as prepare and eat it.

"There's a lot less 'eeew' about vegetables that kids prepare themselves," Robin Krause says. The focus is on recipes like this one, which can be prepared with a peeler, grater, scissors, and, of course, fingers. The term *rösti* comes from a Swiss dish that's made mostly of potatoes. In the Kids Cook kitchen, the rösti cakes are topped with an over-easy egg (from one of the garden's three urban chickens) for added protein.

2 MEDIUM YUKON GOLD POTATOES, PEELED AND GRATED
2 CARROTS, GRATED
½ CUP SLICED SCALLIONS
2 TBSP SNIPPED FRESH CHIVES
½ CUP FINELY GRATED PARMESAN CHEESE
3 LARGE EGGS, LIGHTLY BEATEN
½ TSP SALT
2 TBSP OLIVE OIL

Makes 6 cakes

1 Combine the potatoes, carrots, scallions, chives, cheese, eggs, and salt in a large bowl. Heat some of the oil on a griddle or in large nonstick skillet over medium heat until it shimmers.

2 Working in batches (adding more oil as needed), place the potato mixture in ¼-cup scoops on the griddle and flatten to make cakes. Cook until golden and crispy, 1–2 minutes per side. Drain on paper towels. Serve hot.

MINNESOTA FARMER BANANA BREAD

*From Jean Braatz,
My Minnesota Farmer CSA*

This is a favorite family recipe of Jean Braatz. She and her husband, Dean, operate My Minnesota Farmer CSA in Montgomery, Minnesota, just south of the Twin Cities. The CSA offers locally and naturally grown fruits, vegetables, eggs, grass-fed beef, and other products.

1¾ CUPS UNBLEACHED
   ALL-PURPOSE FLOUR
¼ TSP BAKING POWDER
⅔ CUP SUGAR
1 TSP BAKING SODA
½ TSP SALT
2 LARGE EGGS

⅓ CUP VEGETABLE OIL
3 LARGE OR 4 SMALL VERY RIPE
   BANANAS, MASHED
½ CUP WALNUTS (OPTIONAL)

Makes 1 (9 x 5-inch) loaf

1 Preheat the oven to 350°F. Lightly grease and flour a 9 x 5-inch loaf pan.

2 Blend together the flour, baking powder, sugar, baking soda, and salt in a large bowl. In another bowl, stir together the eggs, oil, and bananas. Create a well in the flour mixture and fold in the banana mixture and walnuts (if using) to form a thick batter.

3 Scrape the batter into the prepared pan and bake until a wooden pick inserted into the loaf comes out clean, about 55 minutes. Turn out of the pan onto a wire rack to cool before slicing.

Edible Fact

Over the past decade, the number of Twin Cities–area residents getting their food through community-supported agriculture (CSA) has nearly tripled, to more than eleven thousand people, reports Minneapolis' *Star Tribune*. Twenty years ago, there were two CSA farms. In 2011, there were eighty-one, according to the Land Stewardship Project, which publishes a CSA directory. Jean Braatz and her husband, Dean, fed 160 families in 2011 throughout the Twin Cities, expanding from about 90 families the previous year.

ORANGE YOGHURT PANCAKES

From Stephanie A. Meyer, writer of the blog Fresh Tart

"These pancakes are my family's favorite breakfast, hands down," says Stephanie A. Meyer. The recipe is via her stepmom's sister-in-law Anne Taylor, who is British, therefore the *h* in the recipe name. Meyer is a home cook, writer, and photographer. Motivated by the belief that all good things come from preparing meals at home, she shares recipes, cooking tips, and photos on her accessible food blog *Fresh Tart,* found at FreshTart.net. She also contributes weekly photos to FoodandWine.com's *Andrew Zimmern's Kitchen Adventures.* Meyer is the organizer of Minnesota Food Bloggers.

1 CUP ALL-PURPOSE FLOUR
½ TSP BAKING POWDER
1 TSP BAKING SODA
¼ TSP SALT
GRATED ORANGE ZEST (OPTIONAL)
½ CUP ORANGE JUICE
¾ CUP WHOLE-MILK PLAIN YOGURT
  (PREFERABLY CEDAR SUMMIT)

1 ORGANIC LARGE EGG
¾ STICK (6 TBSP) UNSALTED
  BUTTER, MELTED
MAPLE SYRUP

Serves 4

1 Stir together the flour, baking powder, baking soda, and salt in a medium bowl. In a small bowl, whisk together the orange zest (if using), orange juice, yogurt, egg, and 4 tablespoons of the melted butter. Stir into the flour mixture until just combined (the batter will be quite thick).

2 Heat a griddle or 12-inch skillet over medium-high heat until quite hot. Brush the pan with some of the remaining melted butter and ladle the batter onto the pan with a spoon into 3-inch pancakes. When the pancakes bubble and are browned, flip and continue cooking until cooked through and browned on the second side, 1–2 minutes. Brush the pan with more melted butter for each batch.

3 Serve warm with maple syrup.

Edible Tip

These pancakes may sound like "health food," but don't be fooled, says Meyer. "They are rich, tender, and completely luscious."

WHITE BREAD SWEET ROLLS

From Kris Woll, Minneapolis writer and Edible Twin Cities *contributor*

These rolls were a Sunday morning staple in Kris Woll's southwest Minnesota home. The recipe was handed down from her mother, who combined a basic bread recipe from the county Extension office with her grandmother's cinnamon- and caramel-coating technique.

Edible Tip

If you'd like, you can make these as frosted rolls: Skip the brown sugar and butter in the bottom of the pan prior to baking. Bake the rolls as directed. Meanwhile, stir together 2 cups confectioners' sugar, ½ stick melted butter, 2 tablespoons milk, and 1 teaspoon vanilla and frost with the icing.

FOR THE ROLLS:
½ CUP WHOLE MILK
3 TBSP SUGAR
2 TSP SALT
11 TBSP UNSALTED BUTTER
1½ CUPS WARM WATER (105–115°F)
1 ENVELOPE ACTIVE DRY YEAST

5½ CUPS ALL-PURPOSE FLOUR
½ CUP GRANULATED SUGAR
1 TBSP GROUND CINNAMON
2 CUPS PACKED LIGHT BROWN
  SUGAR

Makes 12 rolls

1 Heat the milk to just boiling in a medium saucepan over medium heat. Stir in the sugar, salt, and 3 tablespoons of the butter. Set aside and cool to lukewarm.

2 Pour the warm water into a large bowl. Sprinkle the yeast over the surface of the water and stir until dissolved. Add the lukewarm milk mixture and 3 cups of the flour; beat until smooth. Slowly add enough of the remaining 2½ cups flour to make a soft dough.

3 Turn the dough out onto a lightly floured board. Knead until smooth and elastic, 8–10 minutes. Form into a smooth ball. Place in a greased bowl, turning to grease the top of the dough ball. Cover and let rise in a warm, draft-free place until doubled in bulk, about 1 hour.

4 Punch down the dough. Let it rest for 15 minutes in the bowl; then turn it out onto a floured surface and roll it into a rectangle 18 inches long and ¼–½ inch thick.

5 Cut 4 tablespoons of the remaining butter into slices. Sprinkle the surface of the dough generously with the granulated sugar and cinnamon and dot with the butter. Starting at a long side, roll up the dough to form a log.

6 Grease a 9 x 13-inch pan. Sprinkle the bottom of the pan generously with the brown sugar and dot with the remaining 4 tablespoons butter. Slice the dough log crosswise into 12 equal pieces (about 1½ inches thick) and place 3 across and 4 down in the pan. Cover and let rise in a warm, draft-free place until doubled in bulk, about 1 hour.

7 Preheat the oven to 350°F.

8 Bake the rolls until golden brown, about 20 minutes. Turn over onto a sheet of foil to cool.

ROUND DATE BREADS

From Jean Braatz,
My Minnesota Farmer CSA

You've heard of beer-can chicken? This is vegetable-can date bread, a regional riff on traditional, New England–style steamed brown bread. Jean Braatz says her mother-in-law "has made this bread forever" and that it has been in her husband Dean's family for years. Jean and Dean operate My Minnesota Farmer CSA near Montgomery, Minnesota, just south of the Twin Cities. *Note:* To make this dish, you'll need two 20-ounce vegetable cans with both ends removed, thoroughly washed and dried.

1½ CUPS CHOPPED PITTED DATES
2 TSP BAKING SODA
2 TSP UNSALTED BUTTER
1 CUP BOILING WATER
2 CUPS ALL-PURPOSE FLOUR
1 CUP SUGAR

¼ TSP SALT
1 EGG
1 TSP VANILLA EXTRACT
¾ CUP CHOPPED WALNUTS

Makes 2 loaves

1 Heavily grease two 20-ounce vegetable cans (both ends removed). Place the cans on a baking sheet.

2 Combine the dates, baking soda, and butter in a large heatproof bowl. Pour the boiling water over them and let stand until cool.

3 Preheat the oven to 350°F. Add the flour, sugar, salt, egg, and vanilla to the date mixture, and beat vigorously for 1 minute with a wooden spoon. Fold in the walnuts.

4 Scrape the batter into the prepared cans. Bake until a wooden pick inserted into a loaf comes out clean, about 1 hour. Let the bread cool in the cans for 5 minutes before removing. If the bread does not slide out easily, run a knife along the inside of the cans to loosen the loaves and slide them out.

CHAPTER 2

LIGHTER FARE

Some of these so-called appetizers or snacks

could actually be main dishes—the Iron Range Pasty (page 32), for example, or the North Woods Frittata (page 46)—but that's the beauty of a number of these recipes: they are versatile. So feel free to mix and match as you see fit. This chapter also features a few recipes taken from past issues of *Edible Twin Cities*. Though most of the recipes in this book are new, previously unpublished dishes, we are proud to be able to showcase a few items from the magazine.

IRON RANGE PASTY

From Kathy Kiiskinen,
Aurora on the Iron Range

Many Twin Cities residents grew up on the Iron Range, an iron-mining area in the far northern reaches of Minnesota, where a variety of European immigrants settled. Pasties were brought to the Iron Range and other mining areas in Wisconsin and Michigan in the early 1900s by Welsh and Cornish miners and were quickly adopted by other ethnic groups, especially the Finns. Pasties—basically meat pies—were easily packed into lunch pails as a hearty and quick lunch for miners. The miners were creative in warming up the pasties, often putting them on coal-burning stoves or other hot mining equipment. Kathy Kiiskinen, who lives in tiny Aurora on the Iron Range, says, "My dad used to say that when he had a pasty in his lunch box he was the envy of the other men. Some would want to buy his pasty or get my mom to make some for them." These days, pasties are still an Iron Range family favorite. As Kiiskinen says, "When my daughter's family is coming home for a visit, I make sure there are always hot pasties waiting in the oven for their arrival." Kiiskinen makes her own pie dough, but you could use frozen pie dough instead.

FOR THE DOUGH:
1 CUP ALL-PURPOSE FLOUR
PINCH OF SALT
⅓ CUP COOL VEGETABLE
  SHORTENING (IF THE DAY IS
  WARM, CHILL THE SHORTENING
  IN THE FRIDGE FOR A FEW HOURS)

FOR THE FILLING:
1½ CUPS CUBED (1-INCH) POTATOES

½ CUP CUBED (1-INCH) CARROTS
½ CUP CUBED RUTABAGA
  (OPTIONAL)
¼ CUP COARSELY CHOPPED ONION
½ LB LEAN GROUND BEEF
SALT
FRESHLY GROUND BLACK PEPPER
1 TSP MILK

Makes 1 pasty

MAKE THE DOUGH:

1 Combine the flour and salt in a bowl. Cut in the shortening with a fork or pastry blender until the mixture resembles coarse crumbs. With a fork or your hands, mix in 2–3 tablespoons cold water, adding 1 tablespoon at a time, until the dough comes together into a ball.

2 Lightly dust a surface with flour. Dust your hands, a rolling pin, and the dough with flour. Pat the dough down into a round about 1 inch thick. Roll out the dough with the rolling pin, dusting the roller as needed, into a round about 12 inches in diameter.

3 Preheat the oven to 375°F.

4 Mix together the potatoes, carrots, rutabaga (if using), onion, beef, and salt and pepper to taste in a bowl. Place the mixture in the center of the dough round, fold the dough over the filling, and crimp up the edges to seal. Brush with the milk so that it will brown. Make slits on top of the crust.

5 Transfer the pasty to a baking sheet and bake until the veggies are fork-tender, about 1 hour. Eat plain or add melted butter, ketchup, Worcestershire sauce, or warm gravy on top. Pasties freeze well and are also easily heated up in the microwave.

Edible History

The pasty is one of many ethnic dishes that immigrants brought to Minnesota. Germans, Norwegians, Swedes, Finns, Italians—a stunning diversity of Europeans settled here. And, they brought their food and recipes along: pasties, *potica*, lefse, lutefisk, and more.

FUTURE FARM BASIC PESTO

*From Pam Vrieze,
Future Farm Food and Fuel*

Pam Vrieze works for Future Farm Food and Fuel, a company in Baldwin, Wisconsin—not far from the Twin Cities—that operates hydroponic and aquaponic growing systems, producing all-natural vegetables and tilapia fish without harmful chemicals and pesticides. It is a sister company to Baldwin Dairy, which has been family owned and operated in Wisconsin for more than one hundred years, and which provides the energy for the farm's greenhouse by using renewable sources. Future Farm Food and Fuel's vegetables and fish are sold to restaurants, stores, and other businesses in the Twin Cities area.

Edible Tips

Options to have it your way:
• Replace the walnuts or pine nuts with hulled sunflower seeds.
• Nut allergies? Prepare the pesto without nuts and double the amount of Parmesan.
• Replace the basil leaves with fresh cilantro or parsley. Before transferring the pesto to a container, stir in 2 teaspoons fresh lime juice.
• Make a cheese spread: Stir 2 tablespoons of the pesto into 8 ounces of mascarpone cheese (Future Farm uses mascarpone cheese from John Vrieze's Baldwin Dairy). Add seasoned salt to taste.

2 CUPS FIRMLY PACKED FRESH
   BASIL LEAVES
⅓ CUP CHOPPED WALNUTS OR
   PINE NUTS
3 TBSP GRATED PARMESAN CHEESE
2 SMALL CLOVES GARLIC

¼ TSP SALT
¼ TSP FRESHLY GROUND BLACK
   PEPPER
½ CUP EXTRA-VIRGIN OLIVE OIL

Makes about 1 cup

1 Combine the basil, nuts, cheese, garlic, salt, and pepper in a food processor and pulse to a thick paste. With the processor on, add the oil in a slow stream until the mixture is well combined. Transfer to an airtight container. Press plastic wrap directly onto the surface of the pesto (to keep the basil from browning). Cover and refrigerate up to 4 days or freeze up to 2 months.

TWO-CHEESE WALNUT CREAM PIE

From James Norton, cookbook author and online journal editor

This delicious lunch pie is "a locavore adaptation," says James Norton, of Sfoglia di Funghi alla Crema di Noci (Mushroom Pie with Walnut Cream) from *The Silver Spoon*, a classic Italian cookbook. "Our version incorporates Minnesota chèvre and Wisconsin Parmesan to add a bit more depth of flavor without compromising texture or taste." Norton edits *Heavy Table* (HeavyTable.com), which was founded in 2009 as a daily online journal of food and drink in the Upper Midwest.

FOR THE TOPPING:
¾ LB MIXED FRESH MUSHROOMS (CREMINI, PORCINI, SHIITAKE, AND/OR WHITE MUSHROOMS), STEMS REMOVED

FOR THE WALNUT CREAM FILLING:
1 TBSP UNSALTED BUTTER
1 SHALLOT, THINLY SLICED
SCANT 1 CUP WALNUTS, COARSELY CHOPPED
1 LARGE EGG
⅓ CUP CHOPPED UNCURED DELI HAM (PREFERABLY FROM LORENTZ MEATS OR ANOTHER LOCAL MINNESOTA PRODUCER)

¼ CUP FINELY GRATED SARTORI SARVECCHIO OR OTHER AGED PARMESAN-STYLE CHEESE
4 OZ GOAT CHEESE (PREFERABLY STICKNEY HILL DAIRY CHÈVRE)
SALT
FRESHLY GROUND BLACK PEPPER
¼ CUP HEAVY CREAM

FOR THE CRUST:
ALL-PURPOSE FLOUR FOR DUSTING
1 (11 OZ) SHEET PUFF PASTRY, THAWED IF FROZEN
1 TBSP UNSALTED BUTTER
1 CLOVE GARLIC, HALVED

Serves 8–10

PREPARE THE TOPPING:

1 Bring a medium saucepan filled with lightly salted water to a boil. Parboil the mushrooms for 5 minutes. Drain them, pat dry, and slice thickly. Set aside.

MAKE THE WALNUT CREAM FILLING:

2 Melt the butter in a small skillet over medium heat. Add the shallot and cook until softened, about 5 minutes. Remove from the heat.

3 Pulse the walnuts in a food processor until they're a coarse meal. Add the shallot, egg, ham, and Parmesan and process until smooth. Scrape into a bowl. Mix in the goat cheese and season with salt and pepper to taste. Refrigerate for 45 minutes. When ready to bake the pie, remove from the refrigerator and stir in the cream.

MAKE THE CRUST:

4 Preheat the oven to 325°F.

5 Sprinkle a 9-inch pie plate with flour. Unfold the puff pastry and fit it into the pan. Line with parchment paper, fill with dried beans, pie weights, or pie chain, and bake for 10 minutes.

6 Meanwhile, melt the butter in a small skillet and add the garlic halves. Cook for 2–3 minutes. Discard the garlic.

7 Remove the pie shell from the oven and increase the oven temperature to 400°F.

8 Remove the parchment paper and weights and pour the walnut cream filling into the pie shell. Arrange the mushrooms in a decorative pattern on top of the filling. If you have corners (from a square puff pastry) hanging over the side of your pan, you can trim them and put them on top of your filling as edible decorative elements, if desired.

9 Brush the rim of the pastry with the garlic-flavored butter and return the pie to the oven to bake until the filling is mostly set in the center, about 30 minutes.

CHOCOLATE ZUCCHINI BREAD

From Charli Mills, avid camper and Edible Twin Cities *contributor*

Charli Mills grew up in Northern California and learned to cook over a campfire in her father's summer logging camps. She graduated with a degree in writing from Carroll College in Montana but lives in Wisconsin now. She also has worked in marketing communications at Valley Natural Foods co-op in Burnsville. Mills and her family love camping along the rugged North Shore of Lake Superior, about four hours northeast of the Twin Cities, where she honed her best camp-food recipes. This recipe was featured in an article called "Camp Kitchen" in a past issue of *Edible Twin Cities.*

¾ CUP SUGAR
3 TBSP CANOLA OIL
2 LARGE EGGS
1 CUP ORGANIC UNSWEETENED
   APPLESAUCE
2 CUPS ALL-PURPOSE FLOUR
2 TBSP UNSWEETENED COCOA
   POWDER

1¼ TSP BAKING SODA
1 TSP GROUND CINNAMON
¼ TSP SALT
1½ CUPS SHREDDED ZUCCHINI
½ CUP CHOCOLATE CHIPS

Makes 1 loaf

1 Preheat the oven to 350°F. Lightly grease and flour a 9 x 5-inch loaf pan.

2 Combine the sugar, oil, and eggs in a large bowl, and with an electric mixer on low speed, beat until fully blended. Fold in the applesauce until just combined.

3 In a separate bowl, combine the flour, cocoa, baking soda, cinnamon, and salt. Fold the flour mixture into the batter. Stir in the zucchini and chocolate chips.

4 Scrape the batter into the pan and bake until a wooden pick inserted into the bread comes out clean, about 1 hour. Turn out onto a wire rack and let cool completely before slicing and serving.

BUFFALO (BISON) STEAK STRIPS ON A BED OF GREENS

From Mark Ritchie,
Minnesota Secretary of State

Bison meat, commonly known as buffalo meat, has emerged as a popular alternative to beef in Minneapolis and St. Paul, mostly because a growing number of farms in the region are now selling their grass-fed products to Twin Cities food co-ops, grocery stores, restaurants, and caterers. Plus, bison meat is leaner and healthier for you than beef, at least according to some physicians. Mark Ritchie has close family friends who raise delicious bison on Big Shaggy Buffalo Farm near Rochester, which is an hour and a half southeast of the Twin Cities and home of—speaking of physicians—the Mayo Clinic. Ritchie says that his friends Connie and Jim Stannard "take wonderful care of their herd and have turned a beautiful piece of earth into Big Shaggy Farm." (Read more about Ritchie on page 131.)

2 CUPS LOOSELY PACKED GREENS (PREFERABLY ARUGULA), WASHED AND DRIED
⅓ CUP OLIVE OIL
2 CLOVES GARLIC, SMASHED (DO NOT MINCE OR CHOP)
1 SPRIG FRESH ROSEMARY
1 LB THICK-CUT BONELESS BUFFALO (BISON) STEAK, CUT INTO 1-INCH-WIDE STRIPS, AT ROOM TEMPERATURE
1 TSP SALT
¾ TSP FRESHLY GROUND BLACK PEPPER
1 LARGE SHALLOT, SLICED INTO RINGS
1½ TBSP BALSAMIC VINEGAR
1½ TBSP RED WINE VINEGAR

Serves 4

1 Arrange the greens on a large platter.

2 Heat the oil, garlic, and rosemary in a heavy skillet over high heat. Slowly turn the garlic until golden. Discard the garlic and rosemary.

3 Toss the steak strips with ¾ teaspoon of the salt and ½ teaspoon of the pepper. Add the meat to the skillet and cook over high heat, tossing to brown evenly, about 2 minutes. Arrange the buffalo steak strips over the greens.

4 Add the shallot slices to the skillet, along with the balsamic and red wine vinegars and the remaining ¼ teaspoon each salt and pepper, and simmer for 1 minute. Pour the hot shallot dressing over the buffalo strips and greens and serve immediately.

COCKTAIL MEATBALLS, THREE WAYS

*From Amy Lynn Brown
and Heidi Andermack,
Chowgirls Killer Catering*

This recipe has basic cocktail meatballs as its foundation, and three different ways to flavor them. The recipe is a favorite of Amy Lynn Brown and Heidi Andermack, who opened Chowgirls Killer Catering in Minneapolis in 2004. Brown, a Kentucky native, began cooking at age eight when she learned to fry chicken. Andermack, also a talented cook, is a food philosopher, who says, "Cooking is a delicate balance of discipline, intuition, and heart." (Read more about the Chowgirls on page 40.)

FOR THE BASIC MEATBALLS:
1 LARGE EGG
¼ CUP HEAVY CREAM
½ LB GROUND PORK
½ LB GROUND GRASS-FED BEEF
1 CUP FRESH OR DRIED
   BREAD CRUMBS
1 SMALL ONION, FINELY GRATED
⅛ TSP FRESHLY GRATED NUTMEG
⅛ TSP GROUND ALLSPICE
1½ TSP SALT
¼ TSP FRESHLY GROUND PEPPER

FOR THE SWEDISH MEATBALL
GRAVY:
2 TBSP BUTTER
1 TBSP FLOUR
1½ CUPS BEEF STOCK
½ CUP HEAVY CREAM
SALT
FRESHLY GROUND BLACK PEPPER
2 TSP FRESH LEMON JUICE

FOR THE SWEET CHILI SAUCE:
1 CUP CHILI SAUCE (TOMATO-
   BASED, SUCH AS HEINZ)

1 CUP MAYONNAISE
1 CUP PACKED LIGHT BROWN
   SUGAR
1 TBSP GRATED FRESH GINGER
¼ CUP ORANGE JUICE
1 TSP CHOPPED FRESH PARSLEY

FOR THE HONEY, GINGER, AND
LEMON GLAZE:
2 TBSP VEGETABLE OIL
¼ CUP FINELY GRATED FRESH
   GINGER
1 CUP HONEY
1 LEMON, CUT INTO THIN ROUNDS,
   SEEDED
1½ TBSP SOY SAUCE
1 TSP TOASTED SESAME OIL
½ TSP SALT
¾ TSP RED PEPPER FLAKES
1 TBSP CORNSTARCH MIXED WITH
   A LITTLE COLD WATER
1 TBSP FINELY CHOPPED
   CRYSTALLIZED GINGER
2 TSP CHOPPED FRESH CILANTRO

Serves 12

MAKE THE BASIC MEATBALLS:
1 Preheat the oven to 400°F.

2 Beat together the egg and cream in a large bowl. Add the pork, beef, bread crumbs, onion, nutmag, allspice, salt, and pepper, mixing with a wooden spoon or by hand until well combined. Shape into 24 meatballs.

3 Place the meatballs on a wire rack and place the rack on a rimmed baking sheet. Roast until no longer pink in the center and the juice runs clear, 15–20 minutes. Meanwhile, prepare one of the three toppings. The meatballs should still be very hot when they're combined with the topping of choice.

MAKE THE SWEDISH MEATBALL GRAVY:

4 Melt the butter in a skillet over low heat. Stir in the flour and cook until light brown and fragrant, stirring occasionally. Using a wire whisk, slowly add the stock, cream, and a pinch each of salt and pepper. Bring to a boil; then reduce to a gentle simmer and cook for 10 minutes. Stir in the lemon juice. Toss with the hot meatballs.

MAKE THE SWEET CHILI SAUCE:

5 Combine the chili sauce, mayonnaise, brown sugar, ginger, orange juice, and parsley in a medium saucepan. Heat over medium heat, stirring, until the sugar dissolves. Reduce to a low simmer and cook until the sauce is lightly bubbling, shiny, and deep red in color. Toss with the hot meatballs.

MAKE THE HONEY, GINGER, AND LEMON GLAZE:

6 Heat the oil and ginger in a saucepan over medium heat until lightly sizzling. Stir in the honey, lemon rounds, soy sauce, sesame oil, salt, and red pepper flakes and cook over high heat until reduced to a glaze, 5–7 minutes. Discard the lemons. Stir in the cornstarch-water mixture and cook a few minutes more, until thickened. Toss with the hot meatballs and sprinkle with the crystallized ginger. Garnish with the cilantro.

AMY LYNN BROWN AND HEIDI ANDERMACK, CHOWGIRLS KILLER CATERING

Guided by local and organic ideals

Amy Lynn Brown and Heidi Andermack are serious about sustainability; so much so that their entire Minneapolis-based catering business revolves around local and organic ideals.

"If you let the local element guide your cooking, it becomes seasonal and you get the seasonal flavor. Overall, our menus reflect that," says Andermack.

Sprinkled into the Chowgirls mix is a sustainable delivery program that utilizes stainless-steel platters and glass bowls instead of plastic serving pieces that are later thrown away. This requires staff to make an extra trip after the event to collect the items, but they say it's worth it.

"It makes our client's event look more elegant and it's actually better for the environment," says Brown, noting that they also use compostable plates and utensils and offer to compost clients' refuse for a fee.

Started in 2004, the Chowgirls Killer Catering menu offers a range of American comfort foods, vegetarian dishes, and spicy ethnic selections—

many of which can be prepared kosher, gluten-free, vegan, or vegetarian.

Popular comfort foods on the main delivery menu include beef stew, Indian curry, jambalaya, Swedish meatballs, brisket, lasagna, and pulled chicken. Also on the menu are pasta and potato salads, green salads, dips, spreads, and platters.

A separate wedding menu offers a healthy mix of salads, appetizers, sides, entrées, and selections just for kids. In fact, wedding catering encompasses more than half of Chowgirls' business. "We're especially popular with two people who are in love with each other and are in love with sustainability," says Andermack. The other half of their business comes from private parties and corporate events.

Brown worked in co-ops in college and Andermack remembers asparagus hunting in the spring as a child. When Brown and Andermack serendipitously connected in 2003 and started Chowgirls Killer Catering in 2004, organic and locally grown foods

were rarely seen in the catering industry. While other caterers have moved to organic options since then, Brown and Andermack have found creative ways to stay ahead of the competition. "We have the full-service, off-premise catering aspect and composting, whereas many caterers are trying to supplement with a restaurant business that divides their time," says Brown.

In their eight years, Chowgirls Killer Catering has gone from a two-person operation that rented kitchen space on an as-needed basis to a business employing more than seventy people. "I think there's a misperception that it's still just two people," says Brown. "I like that people think we're small and they feel special. Yet, we can still pull off a five-hundred-person event with no problem."

The future is blazing with possibilities, and Andermack says Chowgirls Killer Catering is becoming known as a "tastemaker" in the regional catering industry. "We're fairly close to household-name status," adds Brown.

SAVORY ZUCCHINI PANCAKES WITH
GARLIC YOGURT HERB SAUCE

From Lucia Waston, chef and owner of Lucia's Restaurant, Lucia's Wine Bar, and Lucia's to Go

Twin Cities gardeners will find this recipe especially useful when it's time to harvest all of those zucchinis. As Lucia Watson says, "It is a nice variation when the garden is bursting with zukes!"

Edible Tip

This recipe is good as a vegetarian entrée on a bed of rice pilaf or as a side dish to grilled lamb chops or chicken.

FOR THE GARLIC YOGURT HERB SAUCE:
½ CUP WHOLE-MILK GREEK YOGURT
½ CUP SOUR CREAM
3 TBSP OLIVE OIL
2 TBSP FRESH LEMON JUICE
2 CLOVES GARLIC, MINCED
½ CUP CHOPPED FRESH BASIL
½ CUP CHOPPED FRESH MINT
½ CUP CHOPPED FRESH PARSLEY
SALT
FRESHLY GROUND BLACK PEPPER

FOR THE PANCAKES:
2 CUPS GRATED GREEN AND YELLOW (GOLDEN) ZUCCHINI
¼ CUP GRATED ONION
1 TBSP CHOPPED FRESH BASIL
1 TBSP CHOPPED FRESH PARSLEY
SALT
FRESHLY GROUND BLACK PEPPER
2 LARGE EGGS
2 TBSP ALL-PURPOSE FLOUR
2 TBSP HALF-AND-HALF
GRATED PARMIGIANO-REGGIANO FOR SERVING

Makes 8 large cakes, 4 entrée servings

MAKE THE SAUCE:

1 Combine the yogurt, sour cream, oil, lemon juice, garlic, chopped herbs, and salt and pepper to taste in a food processor. Process just until well blended. Scrape into a bowl and set aside until needed.

MAKE THE PANCAKES:

2 Preheat the oven to 200°F.

3 Combine the zucchini and onion in a large bowl. Fold in the basil and parsley. Season with salt and pepper to taste.

4 Beat the eggs in a medium bowl, sprinkle in the flour, and drizzle in the half-and-half. Beat well with a fork (and don't worry about lumps).

5 Fold the egg mixture into the zucchini, blending thoroughly to create a wet batter.

6 Lightly grease a nonstick griddle and set it over medium-high heat. Working in batches, use a 4-ounce ladle to drop the batter onto the griddle, spreading it gently in a circle. Cook until firm, about 5 minutes. Using a flexible spatula, carefully flip and cook the other side until firm, 3–4 minutes. Remove each batch to an ovenproof plate and keep warm in the oven until ready to serve.

7 Serve the cakes drizzled with the herb sauce and lightly sprinkled with cheese.

MARJ'S CHEESE BALL

From Mark Weber, publisher of
Edible Twin Cities *magazine*

Every Minnesota cookbook needs the quintessential small-town, handed-down recipe, and Marj's Cheese Ball fits the bill, says Mark Weber. This recipe "was bequeathed to my wife, Roma, from her late mother, Helen Given. In turn, Helen got the recipe from her neighbor and longtime friend Marj Cameron." Both lived in Paynesville, Minnesota, population 2,432.

For this cookbook, the recipe has been adapted to use local ingredients, including cream cheese from Organic Valley, of La Farge, Wisconsin; instead of blue cheese spread, a soft blue cheese—AmaBlu St. Pete's Select—from the Caves of Faribault in Minnesota; and sharp cheddar "cold pack cheese food" from Pine River in Wisconsin, where the Lindemann family has been in the dairy business since the 1800s.

2 (8 OZ) PACKAGES CREAM CHEESE, AT ROOM TEMPERATURE
2 (5 OZ) CONTAINERS SHARP CHEDDAR CHEESE SPREAD
1 (5 OZ) CONTAINER BLUE CHEESE SPREAD
3 TBSP WHITE WINE VINEGAR

DASH OF GARLIC SALT
3 TBSP CHOPPED FRESH PARSLEY
1 CUP CHOPPED PECANS

Makes 1 cheese ball (slightly larger than a softball)

1 In a large bowl, using an electric mixer, beat together the cream cheese, cheddar spread, blue cheese spread, vinegar, and garlic salt. Cover and refrigerate the mixture for about 2 hours to stiffen.

2 Shape the mixture into a ball, pat with the parsley, and roll the ball in the pecans. Cover and refrigerate for at least 2 hours to firm up; overnight is better. Serve with assorted crackers and fresh fruit.

MOCK DUCK BANH MI WITH PICKLED TURNIPS AND CARROTS

From Kat Nelson,
Edible Twin Cities *contributor*

This vegan recipe was created by Kat Nelson for the magazine. She explains, "Banh mi is best on a light, airy baguette with a thin crust, rather than a dense, chewy one. If you're a meat eater, you can substitute most any meat—roast pork, pâté, meatballs, chicken, even catfish; all are good options. You will probably have more pickle than you need, but I like to have extra to snack on. If you have a mandoline [slicer], use it to julienne the carrot and turnip." Look for canned mock duck in your local Asian supermarket.

FOR THE PICKLED TURNIPS
AND CARROTS:
1 TBSP SUGAR
1 TSP SALT
½ CUP HOT WATER
½ CUP RICE VINEGAR
1 MEDIUM TURNIP, CUT INTO
⅛-INCH JULIENNE
1 MEDIUM CARROT, CUT INTO
⅛-INCH JULIENNE

FOR THE SANDWICHES:
2 DEMI BAGUETTES
VEGAN MAYONNAISE
1 (8 OZ) CAN MOCK DUCK, SLICED
¼ CUCUMBER, SLICED
1 FRESH JALAPEÑO PEPPER, SEEDED,
DERIBBED, AND JULIENNED
6 SPRIGS FRESH CILANTRO

Makes 2 sandwiches

MAKE THE PICKLED TURNIPS AND CARROTS:
1 Combine the sugar and salt in a medium bowl. Pour the hot water over them and stir to dissolve. Stir in the vinegar. Add the julienned turnips and carrots and toss to coat. Refrigerate for at least 30 minutes.

MAKE THE SANDWICHES:
2 Preheat the oven to 350°F. Place the baguettes directly on an oven rack and heat for 5 minutes. Remove the baguettes from the oven and split horizontally. Spread mayonnaise to taste on the bread. Layer each sandwich with mock duck, cucumber, jalapeño, and drained pickled vegetables to taste. Top with the cilantro and close the sandwich.

Edible History

This versatile sandwich comes to Minnesota from France via Vietnam. It originated during the French colonization of Southeast Asia. The occupying French made portable meals with the ubiquitous long baguette stuffed with pâté, ham, or both, which were both imported and expensive. After the French left in 1954, the Vietnamese adapted the sandwich, adding pickled vegetables and Asian herbs and using smaller baguettes. When they fled their country before and during the Vietnam War, they brought the popular *banh* (pronounced "bun") with them. Here it may be made with barbecued pork or grilled beef.

MOIST DATE NUT BREAD

*From Kate Selner, writer of
the blog* Kate in the Kitchen

Recipe author Kate Selner says she and her older sister were the only two siblings who liked anything with dates. To this day, they remain one of Kate's favorite ingredients in baked goods. Her Twin Cities blog focusing on food and life can be found at KateintheKitchen.com.

2½ CUPS CHOPPED DATES
½ STICK (4 TBSP) UNSALTED BUTTER
1½ CUPS BOILING WATER
½ CUP PACKED LIGHT BROWN SUGAR
1 LARGE EGG
1½ CUPS ALL-PURPOSE FLOUR

1 TSP BAKING POWDER
1 TSP BAKING SODA
1 TSP SALT
1 CUP CHOPPED WALNUTS

Makes 1 (9 x 5-inch) loaf

1 Preheat the oven to 350°F. Grease and lightly flour a 9 x 5-inch loaf pan.

2 Combine the dates and butter in a medium heatproof bowl. Pour the boiling water over them and let stand until cool. When the dates have cooled, stir the mixture to break up any clumps. Fold in the brown sugar and egg until well blended.

3 Combine the flour, baking powder, baking soda, and salt in a separate bowl. Stir the flour mixture into the date mixture until just blended, then stir in the walnuts.

4 Pour the batter into the prepared pan. Bake until a wooden pick inserted in the center comes out clean, about 50 minutes.

5 Let the bread cool for 10 minutes in the pan on a wire rack. Then turn the loaf out onto the rack to cool completely before wrapping tightly in plastic.

MOM'S REFRIGERATOR PICKLES

From Barb Parisien, of St. Paul

Fresh vegetables from the garden or a CSA are truly gifts that Minnesota's northern climate provides, and many rural and urban families alike are able to enjoy these gifts all winter long by preserving a variety of items. Here's a variation on preserving and canning: a recipe for pickles that you keep in the fridge. "This is my ninety-three-year-old mother's recipe," says Barb Parisien, who lives in St. Paul. "I make several batches every year."

7 CUPS SLICED UNPEELED
    CUCUMBERS
1 CUP THINLY SLICED ONION
1 CUP CHOPPED GREEN BELL PEPPER
1 TBSP SALT

1½ CUPS SUGAR
1 CUP CIDER VINEGAR
1 TBSP CELERY SEEDS

Makes 3 pints

1 Place the cucumbers, onion, and bell pepper in a bowl. Sprinkle with the salt and let stand for 1 hour. Drain and distribute the vegetables evenly among 3 pint jars.

2 Stir together the sugar, vinegar, and celery seeds in a bowl until the sugar is partially dissolved. Dividing evenly, pour the vinegar mixture into the jars to cover the vegetables, and refrigerate. You can eat the pickles immediately, but they'll be even better if you wait for at least one week.

NORTH WOODS FRITTATA

*From Jennette Turner,
natural foods educator*

Nothing says the north country quite like wild rice, and indeed many Twin Cities cooks choose wild rice for their dishes, especially when it's in season in the fall. Jennette Turner says that for this earthy frittata you can use any kind of wild or store-bought mushrooms you'd like. In addition, the wild rice can be cooked up to 2 days in advance for convenience.

½ CUP WILD RICE
SALT
2 TBSP BUTTER
1 LB MUSHROOMS, SLICED
½ MEDIUM ONION, DICED
8 LARGE EGGS
2 TBSP MILK OR CREAM
⅛ CUP DRIED CRANBERRIES

¼ TSP FRESHLY GROUND BLACK
    PEPPER
¼ TSP FRESHLY GRATED NUTMEG
¼ TSP GROUND ROSEMARY
½ CUP GRATED PARMESAN CHEESE
CHOPPED PARSLEY, FOR GARNISH

Serves 4

1 Bring 1½ cups water to a boil in a small saucepan over high heat. Add the wild rice and a pinch of salt, reduce the heat to medium, cover, and cook until tender, about 45 minutes.

2 Preheat the oven to 350°F.

3 Melt the butter in a large oven-proof skillet or Dutch oven over medium heat. Add the mushrooms and onion, cover, and cook, stirring occasionally, for 7–8 minutes. Uncover and continue cooking until the liquid evaporates.

4 Combine the eggs, milk, dried cranberries, ½ teaspoon salt, pepper, nutmeg, and rosemary in a large bowl, and mix well. Stir in the cooked rice. Pour the egg mixture over the mushroom-onion mixture.

5 Sprinkle the Parmesan over the top of the eggs. Bake until the eggs have set, about 25 minutes. Let the frittata stand for 5 minutes before cutting into quarters to serve.

Edible Nutrition Tip

Turner says wild rice is a great source of magnesium (1 cup cooked has more than 100 percent of the U.S. recommended daily allowance), a nutrient that helps regulate blood sugar levels, supports the thyroid gland, and maintains nerve health.

JENNETTE TURNER

Improving nutrition habits—with real food

A vintage 1940s stove is at the heart of Jennette Turner's tiny Minneapolis kitchen. The natural foods educator lights up when she describes how she can control the burners and how evenly the oven heats. "That stove has moved with me," she says, noting that it was a gift from her father. "I don't go anywhere unless the stove fits in the kitchen."

It is here that she cooks meals for her family—including her mother, Hazel, her husband, Jon, and her daughter, Jane—and it is here that she develops recipes for Dinner with Jennette, her monthly menu subscription service, as well as for the What's for Supper program at the Wedge Community Co-op in Minneapolis.

Turner is the kind of cook who likes flexible, simple cooking—when one of her recipes calls for onion, it doesn't matter what size, and it doesn't matter if you substitute a leek. Beyond that, there is no caramelizing or other fussy steps. She gives people practical tools to make good nutrition a part of everyday life. "All my stuff is easy," she says. "If the food is good quality, it doesn't need to be doctored up."

Though much of her work happens behind the scenes, Turner has been a constant presence in the natural foods community since training at the Institute for Integrative Nutrition in New York nearly fifteen years ago. At that time, natural foods were not as popular and accepted as they are now, and she participated in the institute's three-year-long nutrition program. But she'd found inspiration abroad. "I lived in France for a while in my early twenties," she says. "I was very influenced by the food culture there—local, fresh, lots of butter!"

She models what she teaches, sipping a ginger lime rooibos tea as she describes some of the basic nutrition and basic cooking lessons she shares with clients. She says for most the key is balanced, planned meals. Getting clients to pay attention to their bodies and food is another goal—Turner helps them tune into rhythm, cycles, and hunger and pay attention to day, night, and seasons. "I do try and help people change gradually, so it's not overwhelming, and I like to be encouraging," she says.

The subtle citrus scent of Turner's tea is a bit like her methods—this natural foods teacher shares tips and insights in ways that invite and inspire. Her goal is to crowd out bad or unhealthy eating habits with real food and focus on balanced meals. "If people are well nourished, then they don't overeat," she says. "The nutrient density of your food matters. Good nutrition isn't just a theory—it really does affect how you feel day in and day out, how much resistance to disease you have, how much energy you have, and what your moods are like."

Turner is deepening her work in the field—moving her focus from individuals to the community at large. In fall 2011, she began studying at the University of Minnesota's School of Public Health to earn her master's degree in community health education with a concentration in public health policy. "My goal is to be able to affect health and nutrition on a wider and deeper scale," she says.

While she studies, she will continue teaching people to eat well and improve their health through individual consultations and small-group and workplace programs. At the core of it all, her mission remains a simple one: "I want people to have nutritious foods, whole food, real food," she says.

CHILES STUFFED WITH FETA

From Nick Schneider, chef and co-founder of Picnic Operetta

In 2009, local chef Nick Schneider collaborated with Scotty Reynolds, director of Mixed Precipitation, in creating Picnic Operetta. This unusual program combines local talent with local ingredients to present open-air opera and a menu of small bites, all offered in Twin Cities community gardens. In 2011, they presented *Alcina's Island* in sixteen Twin Cities garden venues. The two worked closely to make sure that the evening's menu is an integral part of the opera experience. The Chiles Stuffed with Feta recipe came from Schneider as a part of that menu. "This is a classic Greek *meze* [appetizer]," he said. If you can't find Anaheim chiles, "you can pare down a large sweet red pepper to strips for the same purpose."

6 (4- TO 5-INCH) ANAHEIM CHILES OR 10 (3- TO 4-INCH) FRESNO CHILES FOR MORE HEAT

9 OZ SHEEP'S MILK FETA CHEESE, CRUMBLED, AT ROOM TEMPERATURE

2 TBSP EXTRA-VIRGIN OLIVE OIL

2 TBSP WHOLE-MILK PLAIN GREEK YOGURT

1 TBSP MINCED FRESH PARSLEY

¼ TSP DRIED OREGANO

½ TSP GRATED OR MINCED LEMON ZEST

2 EGG YOLKS

KOSHER SALT

FRESHLY GROUND BLACK PEPPER

¼ CUP FINELY GRATED PARMESAN CHEESE

Serves 6

1 Set a broiler rack 6 inches from the broiling element and preheat the broiler. Lightly oil a baking sheet and line with parchment paper.

2 Halve the peppers lengthwise and remove the seeds and ribs. Place the peppers skin-side up on the baking sheet. Broil the peppers until they just begin to blister, 8–10 minutes. Remove the peppers from the baking sheet and set aside to cool.

3 In a medium bowl, using an electric mixer, whip the feta, oil, yogurt, parsley, oregano, lemon zest, egg yolks, and salt and pepper to taste. Stuff each pepper half with some of the filling. Top with Parmesan. Refrigerate until chilled, 20–30 minutes.

4 Preheat the broiler to medium-high.

5 Transfer the stuffed peppers to a baking sheet. Broil the peppers until the filling is bubbling and browning slightly, 4–5 minutes. Serve warm or at room temperature.

Edible Facts

Many Minnesotans were introduced to feta cheese in the 1980s when the University of Minnesota's dairy scientists launched the Minnesota Farmstead Cheese project. Dairy farmers who wanted to develop value-added products worked with university specialists in creating and marketing cheeses made right on their farms. One such cheese was Feta Compli, a delicious version of the classic feta cheese made of sheep's or goat's milk in Greece.

TOMATILLO DIP

*From Lupita Marchan,
Spanish teacher and co-owner
of Living Land Farm*

"This is one of my favorite green dips," says Lupita Marchan. I learned the recipe while visiting family in Mexico several years ago. You can serve it as a dip for your favorite organic corn chips, or it can also be served over beans, eggs, chicken, or anything else that appeals to your taste buds." Marchan leads a double life: she is partner and co-owner with Adam Ellefson of Living Land Farm and a Spanish teacher in nearby Cleveland, Minnesota, so that her summer off dovetails nicely with the busy season on the farm.

Edible Facts

Ingredients from Mexico, such as chayotes, jicamas, and tomatillos, are slowly but surely finding their way onto Minnesota menus. Tomatillos, botanical cousins of the tomato, are sometimes called Mexican green tomatoes. They range in size from a marble to a lime. After the thin paper-like husk is removed and the tomatillo is washed, it can be chopped for use in salads and salsas or cooked in combination dishes. Like the tomato, it is a good source of vitamin C. Many Mexican markets carry both fresh and canned tomatillos.

10 TOMATILLOS, HUSKED AND RINSED
1 TOMATO
1–2 CLOVES GARLIC
1–2 CHILE PEPPERS (SUCH AS JALAPEÑO), SEEDED IF DESIRED
1 ONION
½ BUNCH CILANTRO, TOUGH STEMS REMOVED
⅓ CUP ORGANIC CANOLA OIL
½ CUP ORGANIC PLAIN YOGURT (WHOLE-MILK OR LOW-FAT)
SALT
1½ CUPS FROZEN ORGANIC SWEET CORN, THAWED (OPTIONAL)

Serves 8–10

1 Coarsely chop the tomatillos, tomato, garlic and chiles to taste, onion, and cilantro. Place them in a large bowl and stir in the oil, yogurt, and salt to taste. Stir in the corn (if using). The dip can be stored in a glass jar in the refrigerator for about a week.

WILD RICE, CASHEW, AND ALMOND-STUFFED MUSHROOMS

From Laura Bonicelli, chef and owner of Solo by Bonicelli

Stuffed mushrooms make a great appetizer any time of year, says Laura Bonicelli. In this recipe, "the flavor of the wild rice and the chewiness of the short-grain brown rice work perfectly with the crunch of the almonds and cashews. Add cheese and you have a wonderful filling. I love to keep some of the mixture in the freezer" to use in this quick and popular appetizer. And, Bonicelli says, "I always use hand-harvested Minnesota wild rice."

FOR THE STUFFING:
½ CUP SLIVERED ALMONDS
½ CUP CHOPPED CASHEWS
1 TBSP OLIVE OIL
1 TBSP BUTTER
6 OZ SHIITAKE AND/OR CRIMINI (BABY BELLA) MUSHROOMS, STEMMED AND SLICED
SALT
FRESHLY GROUND BLACK PEPPER
4 SCALLIONS, WHITE AND LIGHT GREEN PARTS ONLY, CHOPPED
1 TSP FRESH THYME LEAVES, CHOPPED
1 CUP WILD RICE, COOKED (DO NOT OVERCOOK)

1 CUP SHORT-GRAIN BROWN RICE, COOKED IN CHICKEN STOCK
1 TBSP CHOPPED FRESH FLAT-LEAF PARSLEY
⅓ CUP GRATED ASIAGO CHEESE
⅓ CUP RICOTTA CHEESE

FOR THE MUSHROOMS:
32 CRIMINI (BABY BELLA) AND/OR WHITE MUSHROOMS, STEMMED
GOOD-QUALITY OLIVE OIL
GOOD-QUALITY BALSAMIC VINEGAR

Serves 8

MAKE THE STUFFING:
1 Preheat the oven to 375°F. Spread the almonds and cashews in a small baking pan and bake until lightly toasted, 4–5 minutes. Remove from the oven, but leave the oven on and increase the temperature to 400°F.

2 Heat the oil in a medium skillet over medium-high heat and add the butter to melt. As soon as the foaming subsides, add the mushrooms and cook until golden brown and soft, 5–6 minutes. Season with salt and pepper to taste. Add the scallions and cook for 1 minute. Add the thyme and cook for 30 seconds.

3 Reduce the heat and stir in the wild rice and brown rice. Stir in the parsley and the toasted nuts. Let cool slightly.

4 Transfer the mixture to a food processor and pulse until chopped, but not fine. Transfer to a bowl and stir in the cheeses. Season to taste.

PREPARE THE MUSHROOMS:
5 Spoon out enough filling to fill a mushroom cap generously and press into a ball. Stuff the filling into the caps and place on a baking sheet.

6 Drizzle the mushrooms with olive oil and bake until the filling is golden brown and the mushrooms are soft, 20–25 minutes.

7 Transfer to a plate and drizzle with balsamic vinegar. Serve warm.

TRUFFLED KETTLE CORN

From Red Stag Supper Club

This fun little snack comes from the Red Stag Supper Club, in the warehouse district of Northeast Minneapolis. The restaurant is a lively new rendition of an old-timey supper club. Its hearty, unpretentious menu features comfort foods from outstate haunts, like fried smelt and stroganoff, made fresh with local and organic ingredients. Here a Supper Club favorite—kettle corn—becomes an elegant bar snack with a sprinkle of truffle salt.

3 TBSP UNSALTED BUTTER TRUFFLE SALT
3 TBSP SUNFLOWER OR PEANUT OIL KOSHER SALT
½ CUP POPCORN KERNELS
1 TBSP SUGAR *Serves 2*

1 Heat the butter in a small saucepan over medium heat until the white milk solids rise to the surface. Remove the saucepan from the heat and gently strain off the clear golden-brownish liquid through a paper towel–lined strainer into a small dish and set aside. (Discard solids.)

2 In a large, heavy-bottomed pot set over medium-high heat, heat the oil until shimmering. Add 3 corn kernels, and when one pops, add the rest of the popcorn kernels. Cover and gently shake the pot over the heat to prevent the kernels from scorching. Continue shaking and cooking until you can't hear any more popping. Remove the pot from the heat and shake a little more. Turn the popped corn into a large bowl.

3 Pour in the clarified butter and toss to coat. Add the sugar and toss. Then add truffle salt and kosher salt to taste and toss again. Serve warm.

Edible Tip

You can find truffle salt in the gourmet section of the supermarket or specialty cookware stores.

CHAPTER 3

SOUPS, SALADS, AND SIDES

Minnesota's short growing season flashes by quickly. Yet somehow, area cooks have managed to invent a surprising wealth of ways to incorporate locally grown produce into delicious dishes. This chapter is a case in point. You'll find recipes for butternut squash soup, grilled romaine lettuce, wild rice cranberry soup, honey-glazed roasted root vegetables, and more. This chapter also shows how, to a large degree, Minnesotans are mindful of the seasons as they plan their menus. Beth Dooley, local cookbook author, writes about this in *The Northern Heartland Kitchen*: "We are governed by the seasons. The weather . . . is dramatic; nature shapes our physical environment as well as our emotional landscape. . . . To eat local means to pay attention to light, temperature, and the land's bounty. When our appetites follow the arc of the sun, we bring balance to our plates."

BUTTERNUT SQUASH SOUP WITH HONEY-THYME HONEYCRISP APPLES

From David Vlach, executive chef of Southview Country Club, West St. Paul

"I've always loved butternut squash soup," says David Vlach. "Along with apples, pumpkins, and the leaves turning color, it is one of the signs of autumn for me." Several years ago, Vlach says, he wanted to serve butternut squash soup as an amuse-bouche. Diners would get only a couple of ounces in an espresso cup to begin their meals, so it had to be intensely flavored and silky-smooth. "As a result, the method for preparing this soup is different in an effort to retain as much flavor and aroma as possible," says Vlach. This recipe becomes a true Minnesota dish with the addition of Honeycrisp apples, which were developed by the University of Minnesota in the early 1960s and are now grown in Minnesota, Wisconsin, and other locations.

Edible History

The Honeycrisp variety was produced in 1960 from a cross of Macoun and Honeygold, as part of the University of Minnesota's apple-breeding program. The original seedling was planted in 1962. These days, as the university reports, Honeycrisp apples feature exceptionally crisp and juicy texture, mildly aromatic flavor, and excellent storage life. The trees have demonstrated good hardiness under normal winter conditions in east-central Minnesota.

FOR THE SOUP:
2 LARGE (2 LB) BUTTERNUT SQUASH, PEELED AND CUT INTO 2-INCH CHUNKS
½ STICK (4 TBSP) COLD UNSALTED BUTTER, CUBED
⅓ CUP PACKED LIGHT BROWN SUGAR
¼ TSP CAYENNE PEPPER
KOSHER SALT
2 CUPS VEGETABLE STOCK
1½ CUPS HALF-AND-HALF
FRESHLY GROUND BLACK PEPPER

FOR THE HONEY-THYME APPLES:
⅓ CUP HONEY
⅓ CUP APPLE CIDER
⅓ CUP WHITE WINE
3 SPRIGS FRESH THYME
1 WHOLE CLOVE
4 HONEYCRISP APPLES, PEELED, CORED, AND CUT INTO ½-INCH CUBES (ABOUT 1 CUP)
THYME SPRIGS OR MINCED FRESH CHIVES, FOR GARNISH

Serves 6

MAKE THE SOUP:

1 Preheat the oven to 375°F. Place the squash in a large roasting pan. Add the butter, brown sugar, cayenne, and 2 teaspoons salt, and toss well. Pour in 1 cup of water and cover the pan with foil. Bake until the squash can be easily mashed with a fork, about 1½ hours.

2 Transfer half of the squash to a blender. Add just enough vegetable stock so that the squash can be pureed. Blend for 2 minutes and pour the puree into a 3-quart saucepan. Repeat the process with the remaining squash and add it to the saucepan along with the half-and-half. Bring to a boil over medium-high heat and cook for 3 minutes, stirring occasionally to prevent it from scorching and sticking to the bottom of the pan. Remove the pan from the heat, taste the soup, and season to taste with salt and pepper. Strain the soup through a fine-mesh sieve into a clean bowl. The soup can be served right away or refrigerated or frozen for later.

MAKE THE HONEY-THYME APPLES:

3 Combine the honey, cider, wine, thyme, and clove in a 1-quart saucepan and bring to a boil. Stir in the diced apples and immediately remove from the heat (do not cook the apples or they will be mushy). Transfer the apples and the poaching liquid to a bowl and refrigerate. The apples can be refrigerated up to 3 days, covered.

TO SERVE:

4 Bring the soup to a boil, stirring constantly. If the soup is too thick, add some of the poaching liquid. Add salt and pepper if desired. Ladle the soup into bowls. Drain the apples and sprinkle on the soup. Garnish with thyme sprigs or chives.

CABBAGE SOUP

*From Jean Braatz,
My Minnesota Farmer CSA*

The Twin Cities area enjoys an especially solid bond that connects rural growers and farm communities with urban markets such as wholesalers, food co-ops, chefs, and caterers. This recipe comes from that rural side. Jean Braatz says, "We love to share our simple foods with people who don't have the time, space, or energy to grow their own, but who are committed to fresh, local food."

2 TBSP UNSALTED BUTTER
¼ CUP FINELY CHOPPED ONION
¼ CUP FINELY CHOPPED CELERY
½ LB POLISH SAUSAGE, SUCH AS
  KIELBASA, SLICED
2½ CUPS CHICKEN STOCK
5 POTATOES, PEELED AND DICED
4 CUPS SHREDDED GREEN CABBAGE

1 CUP FROZEN OR FRESH PEAS
1 TSP SEASONED SALT
⅛ TSP DRIED THYME
⅛ TSP DRIED MARJORAM
SALT
FRESHLY GROUND BLACK PEPPER

Makes 2½ quarts

1 Melt the butter in a large saucepan or Dutch oven over medium-high heat. When the foam begins to subside, add the onion, celery, and sausage and cook, stirring frequently, until the vegetables are soft and the sausage begins to brown, about 8 minutes.

2 Add the chicken stock, potatoes, cabbage, peas, seasoned salt, thyme, and marjoram and bring to a boil. Reduce to a simmer and cook, uncovered, until the vegetables are tender, about 20 minutes. Season to taste with salt and pepper. Serve with warm, crusty bread.

SUE ZELICKSON

An unlikely fan of the local food scene

Sports teams have fans who wear goofy face paint to rally the team and the crowd. The Twin Cities food scene has at least one such fanatic in Sue Zelickson. "There's not a bigger cheerleader of good local food products or fresh food than Sue," says Laurie Crowell, owner of Golden Fig Fine Foods in St. Paul.

Zelickson might seem like an unlikely fan. She doesn't actually cook much and admitted to feeding her two sons quite a few TV dinners while they were growing up. But she is a passionate and tireless advocate of local food. The Golden Valley journalist has edited dozens of cookbooks for fund-raisers. She was the voice of CBS Radio's *Food for Thought*. She's the winner of a James Beard Award in Broadcast Media. She writes a monthly column, "Sue Z Says," for *Minnesota Monthly* magazine. She recently created the Charlie Awards to recognize local chefs and restaurateurs who support nonprofit fund-raising events and efforts in the Twin Cities. Plus, all the proceeds from sales of her Lacey Sue Z. cookie mix go to help kids and families in need at Perspectives,

Inc., and Kids Cafe, for which she has been a board member for more than fifteen years.

She easily traces her love of food and philanthropy to her family, especially her grandmother. "She was a wonderful cook and she was always involved in the community and doing things for charity," Zelickson says. "This was in the 1940s and 1950s. She'd take the streetcar downtown to the Great Northern Market, which isn't there anymore, and bring home fresh produce and ingredients to cook and bake. A lot of my interest came from her."

In 1997, Zelickson helped create Kids Cafe at Perspectives in St. Louis Park. It's a two-thousand-square-foot teaching kitchen for children in kindergarten through grade 6. Jeannie Seeley-Smith of Chaska is president and CEO of Perspectives, Inc.

"Sue's vision was to create a kitchen classroom where kids would learn in a fun and exciting way about cooking and nutrition," Seeley-Smith says. "She loves to teach kids and nurture them through food. Our kids especially lack nurturing and she's always there

to give them a hug. Sue is committed to making a difference in our world with food and using that as her tool to teach and to bring people together."

Zelickson has brought hundreds of women together through her Women Who Really Cook networking organization. Women involved in all aspects of the food business meet to share advice and support. There are now more than 450 members. One of those members is Crowell, of Golden Fig. She describes Zelickson as a connector who is always looking for ways to introduce farmers to restaurants, people to good food, and food producers to retail opportunities.

"I love traveling and checking out new restaurants all over the country. I've been fortunate that I've been able to do that," Zelickson says. "My husband and I have always believed we have to support the restaurants in our community and bring visibility to them."

Crowell sums up Zelickson's contributions succinctly. "It's safe to assume if something great is going on in the food world, Sue had something to do with it."

GINGER ALE–GLAZED CARROTS

From Becky Poss, Edible Twin Cities *contributor*

Carrots are popular in Minnesota because they are hardy root vegetables that can be planted early in the spring and left in the garden until fall, sweetening all the while until you harvest them. Becky Poss is a big fan. "Carrots are not only one of the healthier things on the planet you can consume, but are also a versatile root that transforms itself into a myriad of savory and sweet treats," she wrote in a feature on carrots in a past issue of the magazine.

Edible Tip

Serve with a bottle of smoky chipotle Tabasco sauce on the table—a sprinkle gives these carrots the perfect zing.

2 TBSP UNSALTED BUTTER
1 LB CARROTS (ABOUT 7 MEDIUM),
    CUT ON THE BIAS ¼ INCH THICK
HEAVY PINCH OF KOSHER SALT
1 CUP GOOD-QUALITY GINGER ALE
    (JAMAICAN IS GREAT IF YOU
    LIKE A KICK OF SPICE)

1 TSP CHILE POWDER, PREFERABLY
    ANCHO
1 TBSP CHOPPED FRESH PARSLEY

Serves 4

1 Melt the butter in a large skillet over medium-high heat. Once the foam has subsided, add the carrots, salt, and ginger ale. Reduce the heat to medium, bring to a simmer, cover, and cook until the carrots just begin to soften, 8–10 minutes.

2 Stir the carrots, reduce the heat to low, re-cover, and cook for 5 minutes. Add the chile powder and increase the heat to medium-high, stirring until the ginger ale is reduced to a glorious glaze, about 5 minutes. Serve in a warm dish, sprinkled with the parsley.

CURRIED CRANBERRIES

From Jane Peterson, assistant manager of Ferndale Market, Cannon Falls

This recipe is a lovely change of pace from traditional cranberry sauce that goes great at Thanksgiving time with a free-range turkey, says Jane Peterson, assistant manager of Ferndale Market in Cannon Falls and a member of a farm family in that area. Cannon Falls is about a half hour south of Minneapolis. "As both farmers and shopkeepers, our family's mission at Ferndale Market is simple," Peterson says: "to provide you with the very best local foods. . . . We seek to reconnect folks with the flavors and bounty of local foods."

1 (12 OZ) PACKAGE FRESH
   CRANBERRIES OR 1 (16 OZ)
   PACKAGE FROZEN
1 FINELY CHOPPED APPLE
1 CUP SUGAR
¼ CUP CIDER VINEGAR OR
   RASPBERRY VINEGAR

½ CUP APPLE CIDER OR PORT WINE
½ CUP ORANGE MARMALADE
1½ TSP GROUND CINNAMON
1½ TSP CURRY POWDER
¼ TSP SALT

Serves 8–10

1 Preheat the oven to 325°F. Coat a 2-quart baking dish with cooking spray.

2 Combine the cranberries, apple, sugar, vinegar, cider, marmalade, cinnamon, curry powder, and salt and mix well. Transfer the mixture to the baking dish and cover with foil. Bake until the cranberries are soft, 50–60 minutes.

3 Uncover and let stand at least 10–15 minutes to thicken slightly before serving.

CUCUMBER MELON SALAD

*From Jennette Turner,
natural foods educator*

This is a perfect recipe for late summer, when "you have cucumbers coming out of your ears," says Jennette Turner, who teaches classes at food co-ops and other locations throughout the Twin Cities. Even if you don't have your own garden, visit any neighborhood farmers' market in late summer and you can come away with a stunning bounty of cukes. Turner says this is a tasty accompaniment to grilled pork or chicken and gets even better if you can let it sit in the fridge for 20–60 minutes before serving. (Read more about Turner on page 47.)

FOR THE DRESSING:
3 TBSP SEASONED RICE VINEGAR
1 TBSP SUGAR
¼–½ TSP RED PEPPER FLAKES, TO
    TASTE
PINCH OF SALT

FOR THE SALAD:
1 MEDIUM TO LARGE CUCUMBER,
    PEELED AND THINLY SLICED
½ HONEYDEW MELON OR
    CANTALOUPE, PEELED AND
    CUBED OR BALLED

1 SCALLION, THINLY SLICED
¼ CUP CHOPPED FRESH HERBS (ANY
    COMBINATION OF BASIL, MINT,
    THAI BASIL, AND CILANTRO)
1 SMALL FRESH JALAPEÑO PEPPER,
    SEEDED AND FINELY CHOPPED,
    OPTIONAL
½ CUP UNSALTED ROASTED
    PEANUTS

Serves 4

MAKE THE DRESSING:

1 Combine the rice vinegar, sugar, red pepper flakes, and salt in a small bowl and stir until the sugar is dissolved.

MAKE THE SALAD:

2 Combine the cucumber, melon, scallion, herbs, and jalapeño (if using). Toss well so that all of the ingredients are evenly incorporated. Pour the dressing over the salad and toss. If you have time, let the salad sit in the fridge for 20–60 minutes before serving.

3 Stir in the roasted peanuts right before serving.

Edible Nutrition Tip

According to Turner, cucumbers are a rich source of silica—a mineral essential for healthy connective tissue (tendons, cartilage, and ligaments), muscles, and bones.

EARLY FALL SALAD WITH APPLE DRESSING

From Jennette Turner,
natural foods educator

Summer fades far too soon in Minnesota, but Twin Citians also love the fall. Brisk yet sunny mornings are invigorating. Fall foliage adds natural beauty to the urban landscape. And a refreshing autumn treat is biting into a crisp red Minnesota apple. Thanks to the University of Minnesota's apple-cultivation program, the state produces a variety of delectable apples. This recipe calls for Honeycrisp apples, but the university has developed a number of awesome apples over the years that would also work here, such as Zestar, Haralson, Fireside/Connell Red, and Keepsake to name a few. Jennette Turner says that the dressing makes this main-course salad delicious—a perfect combination of sweet and tart. (Read more about Turner on page 47.)

FOR THE DRESSING:
1 CUP APPLE CIDER
⅛ TSP SALT
2–3 TSP CIDER VINEGAR
⅛ TSP FRESHLY GROUND BLACK
    PEPPER
¼ CUP OLIVE OIL

FOR THE SALAD:
1 HEAD LEAF LETTUCE, CHOPPED
½ HEAD RADICCHIO, SLICED
    (OPTIONAL)

2 HONEYCRISP APPLES, CORED
    AND CUBED
1 CUP RED SEEDLESS GRAPES,
    HALVED
1 CUP WALNUTS, TOASTED AND
    COARSELY CHOPPED
4 OZ CHEDDAR CHEESE, CUBED
½ LB COOKED TURKEY BREAST,
    CUBED
¼ CUP THINLY SLICED RED ONION
    OR 3 TBSP MINCED FRESH CHIVES

Serves 4

MAKE THE DRESSING:

1 Bring the apple cider and salt to a boil in a small saucepan over medium-high heat. Cook until the liquid is reduced to ¼ cup, about 8 minutes.

2 Remove from the heat and transfer to a small bowl or jar. Add the vinegar to taste and pepper. Whisk in the olive oil (or shake well in a jar).

MEANWHILE, MAKE THE SALAD:

3 Combine the lettuce, radicchio (if using), apples, grapes, walnuts, cheddar, turkey, and red onion in a large salad bowl. Add the dressing and toss well to coat.

Edible Nutrition Tip

Bioavailable melatonin has been discovered in walnuts, says Turner. This hormone (produced in the human body by the pineal gland) helps to induce and regulate sleep, and also functions as an antioxidant.

FARRO PILAF WITH GOLD BEETS

From Kate Selner, writer of the blog Kate in the Kitchen

Combining a growing love of whole grains and beets was the inspiration behind this recipe, says Kate Selner. Golden beets are a favorite of hers; she explains that they are less earthy than red beets, and so pretty on a plate. With the red pepper, plump farro, and dabs of creamy goat cheese, "this dish was a fall feast for both mouth and eye," she says. She notes that farro can be cooked like any other grain, with a 2:1 ratio of water to grain; 1 cup uncooked will yield the amount needed for this recipe. It should be tender to the bite, not too firm, with a texture similar to barley. Be sure to rinse it thoroughly in a sieve prior to cooking; it can be very dusty. Kate's Twin Cities blog focuses on food and life can be found at KateintheKitchen.com.

1 TBSP OLIVE OIL
1 RED BELL PEPPER, SEEDED, DERIBBED, AND DICED
1 SMALL SHALLOT, DICED
2 CLOVES GARLIC, MINCED
BEET GREENS (FROM THE BEETS), TOUGH RIBS REMOVED, COARSELY CHOPPED
3 CUPS COOKED FARRO

3 LARGE GOLDEN BEETS, ROASTED, PEELED, AND DICED
SALT
FRESHLY GROUND BLACK PEPPER
½ CUP CRUMBLED FETA OR GOAT CHEESE
⅓ CUP PECAN PIECES

Serves 4

1 Heat the oil in a deep, straight-sided 10-inch skillet (with a tight-fitting lid) over medium-high heat until shimmering. Add the red pepper and cook until soft, about 5 minutes. Add the shallot and cook until soft and slightly golden, 5–8 minutes. Add the garlic and cook until just fragrant, about 30 seconds.

2 Add the beet greens and stir well, until they're just barely wilted. Stir in the cooked farro, beets, and ⅓ cup of water. Cover the skillet, reduce the heat to low, and cook, stirring occasionally, until heated fully through. Season to taste with salt and pepper. Serve warm, topped with feta and pecans.

HONEY-GLAZED ROASTED ROOT VEGETABLES

From Beth Dooley,
Minneapolis food writer

This sweet twist on an old-fashioned favorite tosses together the best of the root cellar. Midwestern sweet potatoes have a drier flesh and are less sweet than their southern cousins. Turnips—and the ubiquitous rutabaga, aka baga—give this honey-kissed dish a bitter balance. This is great alongside pork chops or roast chicken.

2 MEDIUM PARSNIPS, PEELED AND CUT INTO 2-INCH PIECES

1 LARGE CARROT, PEELED AND CUT INTO 2-INCH PIECES

1 SMALL TURNIP, PEELED AND CUT INTO 2-INCH PIECES

1 CUP PEELED AND CUBED RUTABAGA

1 MEDIUM SWEET POTATO, PEELED AND CUT INTO 2-INCH PIECES

1 SMALL YELLOW ONION, COARSELY CHOPPED

2 TBSP SUNFLOWER OR VEGETABLE OIL

1 TBSP COARSE SALT

2 TBSP HONEY

2 TBSP UNSALTED BUTTER, MELTED

Serves 4–6

1 Preheat the oven to 400°F.

2 Toss together the parsnips, carrot, turnip, rutabaga, sweet potato, and onion in a large bowl. Add the oil and toss to coat. Sprinkle with the salt and toss again. Spread the vegetables out in a single layer without touching on 2 heavyweight baking sheets.

3 Roast the vegetables, shaking the pans occasionally, turning the vegetables with a spatula to keep them from sticking, until they develop a light crust and are tender, 40–50 minutes.

4 Meanwhile, stir together the honey and butter.

5 Brush the vegetables with the honey butter, return to the oven, and roast until the vegetables are thickly glazed, about 5 minutes.

MINNESOTA-GROWN GRILLED ROMAINE LETTUCE WITH SEA SALT

From Doug Peterson, president of the Minnesota Farmers Union

This easy recipe is from Doug Peterson, who heads up the Minnesota Farmers Union, a nonprofit, grassroots, membership-based group. Since 1942, the organization has worked to protect and enhance the economic interests and quality of life of family farmers and ranchers and rural communities. The group provides a voice for its members in both St. Paul and Washington, D.C. Serve this lettuce alongside the Grilled Country Chicken (page 99).

2 HEADS ROMAINE LETTUCE (PREFERABLY MINNESOTA-GROWN), HALVED LENGTHWISE

SUNFLOWER OIL (PREFERABLY MINNESOTA-GROWN)

SEA SALT (PREFERABLY REDMOND NATURAL REAL SALT)

BITTERS

Serves 4–6

1 Preheat a grill to medium-high heat.

2 Combine the romaine and enough sunflower oil to coat in a large bowl. Add sea salt to taste (but don't overdo it) and toss well. Add several drops of bitters and toss again.

3 Grill over indirect heat (the lettuce must retain crispness, but some charring should be present for maximum taste). Serve hot.

Edible Facts

Minnesota, like many midwestern states, has lots of farms. For example, currently the state's Department of Agriculture lists eighty-one thousand farm families in Minnesota. Plus, the state has a robust organic agriculture component. The U.S. Department of Agriculture reports that in 2008 the state had 543 certified-organic farm operations, with 133,393 acres of organic crops.

LEMONY GARLIC WHITE BEANS

From Kate Selner, writer of the blog Kate in the Kitchen

Quick, simple meals that can come from your own pantry are specialties for Kate Selner, a contributor to *Edible Twin Cities*. She says she sometimes challenges herself to see just how nutritious a meal she can make with what she has on hand. These easy beans are one of those recipes. They only get better with time in the refrigerator, Selner says, but they rarely last that long. They can be eaten alone, as a topping for toasted bread, or as a filling for an omelet. Kate's Twin Cities blog focuses on food and life and can be found at KateintheKitchen.com.

1 LEMON
1 (15 OZ) CAN GREAT NORTHERN
    OR CANNELLINI BEANS, RINSED
    AND DRAINED
½ CUP GRAPE TOMATOES, HALVED
    (MORE IF DESIRED)
2–3 TBSP CHOPPED FRESH BASIL
OLIVE OIL

2 TSP FRESH THYME LEAVES
1 TSP RED PEPPER FLAKES
2 CLOVES GARLIC, THINLY SLICED
SALT
FRESHLY GROUND BLACK PEPPER

Serves 4–6

1 Grate the zest from half of the lemon. Squeeze all of the juice.

2 Combine the beans, tomatoes, basil to taste, and lemon zest in a medium bowl.

3 Warm 1 tablespoon of oil and the thyme and pepper flakes in a small skillet over low heat. When the oil is hot and the leaves are sizzling slightly, add the garlic slices and cook gently until the garlic is lightly browned. Stir in the lemon juice. Pour the dressing over the beans and stir gently to combine.

4 Mash some of the beans slightly and season the salad with salt and black pepper to taste. Add more oil if the beans seem too dry. Chill for 1–2 hours. Stir again before serving.

POACHED PEARS

*From Beth Dooley,
Minneapolis food writer*

Pears grow especially well along the shores of Lakes Superior and Michigan and come into season in midfall. These poached pears make a lovely side dish, and since they can be made ahead of time and served at room temperature or chilled, what could be easier? This recipe is from Beth Dooley, author of *The Northern Heartland Kitchen.* She has covered the local food scene for more than twenty-five years and is the restaurant critic for *Mpls.-St. Paul* magazine. She also writes for the Taste section of Minneapolis's *Star Tribune* and appears regularly on KARE-TV, the NBC affiliate in the Twin Cities.

Edible Tip

For this recipe, it is best if the pears are not too ripe.

6 MEDIUM PEARS, SUCH AS
  BARTLETT
1 CUP SWEET WHITE WINE, SUCH
  AS RIESLING
½ CUP SUGAR
1 LEMON, SLICED

1 CINNAMON STICK
2 WHOLE CLOVES
2 TBSP CRÈME FRAÎCHE

Serves 6

1 Peel the pears, and then core each pear from the blossom end with a melon baller, scooping the pear to within ½ inch of the stem, and leaving the stem intact.

2 Combine ½ cup of water, the wine, and the sugar in a heavy saucepan large enough to hold all the pears upright. Bring to a boil over medium heat, stirring to dissolve the sugar. Reduce the heat to medium-low and add the lemon slices, cinnamon stick, and cloves. Stand the pears, blossom-end down, in the pan, and simmer until the pears are soft when pierced with a sharp knife, about 20 minutes.

3 Using a slotted spoon, transfer the pears to a plate and tent with foil to keep warm. Increase the heat to high and cook the sauce until it is reduced by half, 10–15 minutes. Strain the sauce through a medium-mesh sieve. Swirl in the crème fraîche.

4 Pour a little of the sauce onto individual plates and set a pear on each pool of sauce, passing the remaining sauce separately at the table.

SUMMER GRATIN

*From Beth Dooley,
Minneapolis food writer*

This dish, which marries the best and sweetest summer vegetables commonly found in Twin Cities markets, comes together quickly and is very forgiving, says Beth Dooley, author of *The Northern Heartland Kitchen*. Don't worry about over-baking: the longer it lingers in the oven, the more the vegetables melt into each other. Leftovers are wonderful stuffed into a pita sandwich, tossed with pasta, or even topped with a poached egg for a light dinner.

Edible Tip

Make this vegan by substituting chopped Kalamata olives or toasted breadcrumbs for the cheese.

4 TBSP EXTRA-VIRGIN OLIVE OIL
4 MEDIUM WAXY (BOILING) POTATOES (ABOUT 1 LB), PEELED AND CUT INTO ½-INCH-THICK ROUNDS
SALT
FRESHLY GROUND BLACK PEPPER
1 LB EGGPLANT (1 LARGE ITALIAN EGGPLANT OR 2–3 ASIAN OR SMALLER WHITE EGGPLANTS), CUT INTO ½-INCH-THICK ROUNDS

4 SMALL ZUCCHINI (ABOUT 1 LB), CUT INTO ROUNDS
3 MEDIUM RED ONIONS, CUT INTO ½-INCH-THICK ROUNDS
4 PLUM TOMATOES, CUT INTO ½-INCH-THICK ROUNDS
4 CLOVES GARLIC, SMASHED
1 CUP SHREDDED PARMESAN CHEESE

Serves 6–8

1 Preheat the oven to 375°F. Lightly grease a 9 x 13-inch baking dish with 1 tablespoon of the oil.

2 Layer the potatoes over the bottom of the dish and sprinkle with salt and pepper.

3 Toss together the eggplant, zucchini, onions, tomatoes, garlic, and remaining 3 tablespoons oil in a large bowl. Arrange the vegetables over the potatoes. Cover the baking dish tightly with foil.

4 Bake for 30 minutes. Remove the foil, sprinkle with the cheese, and continue baking, recovered with the foil, until the vegetables are cooked through and the cheese is a rich golden brown, 45–55 minutes. Serve hot or at room temperature.

POTATO GRATIN

*From Ann L. Burckhardt,
food writer and cookbook author*

We Minnesotans like to consider ourselves a cultured group of epicurean experts, but, frankly, we also have a basic meat-and-potatoes side to us. This recipe offers the perfect accompaniment for slow-roasted or grilled meats, says Ann L. Burckhardt, a local food writer who lives in Edina. Burckhardt, who was a writer and editor for twenty-four years at Minneapolis' *Star Tribune*, is the author or editor of eighteen cookbooks.

1 LB WAXY (BOILING) POTATOES,
  PEELED AND SLICED INTO
  ¼-INCH-THICK ROUNDS
1 SMALL CLOVE GARLIC, MINCED
SALT
FRESHLY GROUND BLACK PEPPER
½ LB SLICED MUSHROOMS,
  PREFERABLY SHIITAKE OR
  PORTOBELLO

1 CUP HEAVY CREAM
1 TBSP UNSALTED BUTTER, CUBED,
  PLUS MORE FOR GREASING THE
  DISH

Serves 4

1 Preheat the oven to 300°F. Lightly grease a 1½-quart baking dish with butter.

2 Lay half the potatoes in the baking dish, overlapping them if necessary and sprinkling the layer with half of the garlic, and salt and pepper to taste. Top the potatoes with the mushrooms. Top with the rest of the potato slices, sprinkling them with the rest of the garlic, and salt and pepper to taste.

3 Slowly pour the cream over the vegetables, allowing them to absorb it a little at a time. Dot with the 1 tablespoon butter and cover with heavy-duty foil.

4 Bake the gratin for 1½ hours, removing the foil for the last 15 minutes to brown the top. Serve hot or at room temperature.

SPRING PEA SOUP

From Laura Bonicelli, chef and co-owner of Solo by Bonicelli

This is a seasonal soup from Laura Bonicelli, who serves a variety of clients through her fresh meal delivery service—from those too busy to cook, to those trying to lose weight, to new moms, to individuals recovering from illness. "As a chef in Minnesota, I wait all winter for the spring vegetables to come to the markets. They usher in the bountiful summer season of locally grown food." Bonicelli describes this recipe as "a French-style soup, and it's always a surprise to clients because they think of pea soup as being heavy. Like a vichyssoise, the soup can be served at room temperature."

2 TBSP UNSALTED BUTTER
2 TBSP EXTRA-VIRGIN OLIVE OIL
1 LARGE LEEK, WELL WASHED, DICED (WHITE AND LIGHT GREEN PARTS ONLY)
1 LARGE OR 2 SMALL HEADS BIBB LETTUCE, COARSELY CHOPPED (ABOUT 6 CUPS)
¼ CUP COARSELY CHOPPED FLAT-LEAF PARSLEY
4 CUPS CHICKEN STOCK
2 CUPS FRESH GREEN PEAS
SALT
FRESHLY GROUND BLACK PEPPER
½ CUP HEAVY CREAM

Serves 4

1 Melt the butter with the olive oil in a 4-quart saucepan over medium heat. When the foam subsides, add the leek and cook slowly until soft but not browned, 8–10 minutes.

2 Add the lettuce and parsley and cook, stirring constantly, until completely wilted, 1–2 minutes. Add the stock and peas, increase the heat, and bring to a boil. Reduce to a simmer and cook, uncovered, for 10 minutes.

3 Remove the pan from the heat and, using an immersion blender, puree until smooth. Return the soup to the heat, season with salt and pepper, and stir in the cream. Heat the soup to hot but not boiling. Taste for seasoning. Serve hot.

WARM BACON AND SPINACH SALAD WITH MAPLE MUSTARD DRESSING—THE BEST DRESSING EVER

*From Jennette Turner,
natural foods educator*

Jennette Turner says she loves bacon from Pastures A Plenty, a sustainable, family-run farm in Kerkhoven, in western Minnesota. Twin Citians can buy Pastures A Plenty products from Clancey's Meats in the Linden Hills neighborhood of Minneapolis (Kristin Tombers of Clancey's is profiled on page 87) and area food co-ops. Turner says this dish is "an amazingly delicious way to use the vitamin D–rich fat from cooking bacon."

¾ LB BACON

1 LB YUKON GOLD POTATOES, PEELED AND CUT INTO 1-INCH CUBES

2 TBSP WINE VINEGAR, PREFERABLY WHITE

1 TBSP DIJON MUSTARD

2 TSP MAPLE SYRUP

4 CUPS LOOSELY PACKED FRESH SPINACH

4 HARD-BOILED EGGS, PEELED AND SLICED INTO ROUNDS

1 MEDIUM TOMATO, CHOPPED

¼ CUP THINLY SLICED RED ONION

Serves 4

1 Cook the bacon in a skillet over medium-high heat until crisp. Drain on paper towels. Strain the bacon fat through a fine-mesh sieve and reserve.

2 Cook the potatoes in a medium saucepan of lightly salted boiling water until just tender, 10–12 minutes. Drain and set aside.

3 Blend together the vinegar, mustard, and maple syrup in a small bowl. Whisk in ⅓ cup of the reserved bacon fat until completely emulsified, about 30 seconds.

4 Toss the spinach with the potatoes, egg slices, tomato, and onion. Break the bacon slices into pieces and add them to the salad. Pour the dressing over the salad and toss to coat. *Note:* if you want to garnish the salad with all or some of the egg slices rather than mix them into the salad, that's just fine.

Edible Nutrition Tip

Turner says that bacon is a great source of the B vitamin choline, which is a building block for acetylcholine—a neurotransmitter that is needed for memory and learning ability.

GREG AND MARY REYNOLDS, RIVERBEND FARM

From physics and psychotherapy to arugula and zucchini

Greg Reynolds grew up on a farm. The family farm went to his brother, and Reynolds went on to a degree in physics and a job as an engineer of laser-based measurement applications. But the yen for farming didn't go away. In 1994, he and his wife, Mary, purchased thirty acres just west of Delano—about thirty miles from the Twin Cities.

Located on the North Fork of the Crow River, the farm has sandy soil, low in organic matter, which made it a challenge for organic farming. At the time the Reynoldses purchased it, the farm and its soil had been through twenty-five years of corn crops that had depleted whatever organic matter was left in the soil.

Reynolds kept his day job for five more years, and Mary continued to work as a psychotherapist as they brought the farm up to the levels required to grow certified organic crops. They asked a neighbor to plant alfalfa, which benefitted the soil while providing a small cash crop. They planted sorghum–Sudan grass and soybeans, which also put nutrients back into the soil. "After about five years of organic management, it seemed like the soil came back to life," the website notes.

The first certified organic crops, squash and tomatoes, were sold to a co-op in Buffalo, Minnesota, which remains one of Riverbend Farm's primary customers. They also started a community-supported agriculture (CSA), with members subscribing in the spring to receive a weekly box filled with seasonal vegetables. By the 2011 growing season, the CSA had grown from its original four members to eighty. In addition, the farm now sells produce to a range of independent restaurants and co-op groceries in the Twin Cities. If you are a fan of local and organic food, chances are you've already tasted the produce grown on Riverbend Farm.

Marshall Paulsen, chef for the Birchwood Cafe in Minneapolis, is a loyal Riverbend Farm customer. "I communicate directly with Greg. I know him personally. I know his family. I've been in his fields," Paulsen says. "I think the biggest thing is trust. When I get the food [delivered] from Riverbend Farm in the back door, I trust that it will have character, vibrancy, color, and great flavor. I know it was grown with passion and hard work. I think you can taste that."

Problem solving is the common element in Reynolds's careers as physicist and farmer, he says. But organic farm-

ing offers more difficult problems to solve. "With the lasers, if you get things to line up, it will work. In farming, you can have everything lined up and something will still go wrong." Crop rotation and cultivation kill weeds, rather than chemical pesticides. Most insects are left alone because they pollinate crops and eat other insects, with grassy habitat left between the vegetable beds. (Incidentally, according to Reynolds, research shows that insect damage actually raises the level of antioxidants in vegetables!)

Another major difference between Riverbend Farm and typical commercial farms is the variety of crops the Reynoldses grow on their thirty acres. Nearly half of all acreage in the United States is planted for corn and soybeans.

By contrast, Riverbend Farm produces literally dozens of different crops each year. The growing season is divided into thirds, each "mini-season" producing its own bounty: arugula to zucchini in early summer; basil and beans to watermelon in midsummer; and apples to winter squash in late summer and fall. As Reynolds says, "You need to have a lot of things for CSA."

SWEET AND SAVORY QUINOA SALAD

From Jenny Breen, chef and co-owner of Good Life Catering, Minneapolis

How about a lovely, cool, summery grain salad for those hot, humid July and August days in Minnesota? That's what Jenny Breen had in mind when she created this recipe, but, as she says, she wanted "something other than tabbouleh. Nothing against that wonderful dish, but there's more to life than mint and parsley." Breen says, "It is a joy to cook with sesame oil—its nutty flavor stands up to cooking and adds a wonderful layer of complexity to any dish. The fresh notes of honey and fruit juice balance the tartness of the mustard, and the crisp greens and tangy dried fruit are an unusual match finished by the sweet crunch of the nuts." An added benefit to quinoa is that it's packed with as much protein as it is with warm, nutty flavor, and it cooks very quickly.

FOR THE SALAD:
2 CUPS COOKED QUINOA
1 LARGE BUNCH SWISS CHARD, STEMS REMOVED, LEAVES CHOPPED
½ CUP THINLY SLICED SWEET ONION OR SCALLIONS
1 CUP WALNUTS OR PECANS, TOASTED AND CHOPPED
½ CUP DRIED FRUIT (DICED APRICOTS OR CURRANTS)

FOR THE ORCHARD DRESSING:
½ CUP RICE VINEGAR
¼ CUP TOASTED SESAME OIL
¼ CUP SAFFLOWER OR CANOLA OIL
¼ CUP ORANGE OR APPLE JUICE
2 TBSP TAMARI
2 TBSP HONEY
2 TBSP DIJON MUSTARD
1 TSP SALT

Serves 10–12

1 Combine the quinoa, chard, onion, nuts, and dried fruit in a large salad bowl.

2 Whisk together the vinegar, oils, orange juice, tamari, honey, mustard, and salt in a small bowl.

3 Toss the salad with about ¾ cup of the dressing, or to taste, and mix well. Refrigerate until chilled.

4 Serve salad as is or over a bed of greens.

Edible Tip

Breen offers this idea for getting the whole family involved with creating this dish. In addition to chopping chard leaves, this recipe has a lot of room for variation, so encourage the kids to taste and describe the flavors and come up with other ingredients to add or to use as substitutes for those listed.

WILD RICE AND APPLE SALAD

From Beth Dooley,
Minneapolis food writer

As author Beth Dooley explains in her latest book, "True wild rice isn't rice at all but an annual aquatic cereal grass that produces an edible seed." Dooley's cookbook, *The Northern Heartland Kitchen*, was published in the fall of 2011 by the University of Minnesota Press. This recipe, Dooley says, calls for hand-harvested rice, available in most grocery stores, natural food co-ops, and farmers' markets. "It's so tasty you don't really need more than a pat of butter and a few chopped herbs," she says. Leftovers freeze nicely. Further, she says, this salad makes great use of leftover wild rice for a light luncheon treat or hearty side dish. It also holds up nicely on a holiday buffet.

FOR THE WILD RICE:
1 CUP WILD RICE, WELL RINSED UNDER COLD RUNNING WATER
3 CUPS WATER OR STOCK
1 PAT BUTTER
CHOPPED HERBS OF YOUR CHOICE (THYME AND PARSLEY WORK WELL)

FOR THE CIDER VINAIGRETTE:
1 TBSP APPLE CIDER
1 TBSP CIDER VINEGAR
1 TSP DIJON MUSTARD
1 TSP HONEY
¼ CUP WALNUT OR VEGETABLE OIL

FOR THE SALAD:
1 LARGE TART APPLE, CORED AND CUT INTO ¼-INCH CHUNKS
1 STALK CELERY, COARSELY CHOPPED
1 SMALL RED ONION, COARSELY CHOPPED
¼ CUP DRIED CRANBERRIES
SALT
FRESHLY GROUND BLACK PEPPER
¼ CUP WALNUTS, TOASTED AND CHOPPED

Serves 6

MAKE THE WILD RICE:
1 Combine the wild rice, water, butter, and herbs in a large saucepan. Bring to a boil over high heat. Reduce to a simmer and cook until the wild rice is tender but not mushy, 20–30 minutes.

MEANWHILE, MAKE THE VINAIGRETTE:
2 Whisk together the cider, vinegar, mustard, and honey in a small bowl. Whisk in the oil in a slow, steady stream.

ASSEMBLE THE SALAD:
3 Toss together the cooked wild rice, apple, celery, onion, and cranberries with the vinaigrette. Season with salt and pepper to taste. Scatter the toasted walnuts over the top.

Edible History

Beth Dooley reports that Minnesota is the center of the biodiversity of all wild rice and has more than sixty thousand acres of natural wild rice growing throughout the state's northern lakes and rivers in the heart of Ojibwe country. Sacred to the Ojibwe, wild rice continues to play a central role in contemporary Native American culture in communities in Minnesota, Wisconsin, and Michigan.

WILD RICE CRANBERRY SOUP

*From Paulette Mitchell,
cookbook author, food writer,
and television personality*

Wild rice and cranberries are favorites in Minnesota and the Upper Midwest—products of the northern climate and of the many lakes and bogs that dot the landscape. Wild rice is appreciated for its nutty flavor. That's brought home in this soup recipe, which creatively adds a fried sage garnish that is colorful, crunchy, and tasty. Paulette Mitchell, who lives in Edina, is the author of thirteen cookbooks and known globally for her quick-to-prepare recipes with gourmet flair. The author of the award-winning *15-Minute Gourmet* cookbook series, she is also a video producer of Telly Award–winning travel and culinary videos as well as a media spokesperson, freelance writer, culinary speaker, cooking instructor, and television personality.

FOR THE SOUP:
½ STICK (4 TBSP) UNSALTED
   BUTTER
1 CARROT, FINELY CHOPPED
1 STALK CELERY, FINELY CHOPPED
½ CUP FINELY CHOPPED ONION
3 TBSP ALL-PURPOSE FLOUR
3 CUPS CHICKEN STOCK
1½ CUPS COOKED WILD RICE
½ CUP DRIED CRANBERRIES
1 CUP HALF-AND-HALF

2 TBSP DRY SHERRY (OPTIONAL)
FRESHLY GROUND PEPPER
SALT

FOR THE FRIED SAGE GARNISH:
EXTRA-VIRGIN OLIVE OIL
4–6 FRESH SAGE LEAVES
FINE SALT

Serves 4–6

MAKE THE SOUP:

1 Melt the butter in a large Dutch oven over medium heat. When the foam subsides, add the carrot, celery, and onion and cook, stirring occasionally, until the carrot is tender and the onion translucent, about 8 minutes.

2 Sprinkle in the flour and stir briskly until smooth. Slowly pour in the stock, whisking constantly to prevent lumps. Increase the heat to medium-high and stir as the soup thickens, about 5 minutes.

3 Stir in the wild rice and cranberries. Reduce to a simmer, cover, and cook, stirring occasionally, until the cranberries are softened and plumped, about 15 minutes. Stir in the half-and-half, dry sherry (if using), and pepper to taste. Stir occasionally until warmed through. Season with salt and pepper to taste.

MAKE THE FRIED SAGE GARNISH:

4 Pour ½ inch of oil into a small saucepan or skillet and heat over medium-high heat. When a drop of water sizzles in the oil, add the sage leaves and fry for about 15 seconds, turning occasionally with a slotted spoon or tongs. (Don't let the leaves brown, or they'll become bitter.) Transfer the leaves to a paper towel–lined plate. The leaves will crisp as they cool. Sprinkle lightly with fine salt.

5 Serve the soup garnished with the sage.

CHAPTER 4

MAINS

Most Minnesota kitchens are no-nonsense
places where simple food preparations are favored over more elaborate
approaches. That's not to say our chefs and home cooks lack creativity.
Indeed, they can be quite inventive; they just sometimes choose not to over-
think things. This chapter offers a good-looking roster of uncomplicated,
delicious options for Minnesota-themed entrées, such as Venison Loin in
Pancetta with Cranberries, Turkey Meatloaf, Minnesota Harvest Salad, and
Snowy Winter Lentil Stew. Just the name of this last one has us reaching for
our cross-country skis.

BEEF BRAISED IN COCONUT MILK

From Stephanie A. Meyer,
writer of the blog Fresh Tart

Stephanie A. Meyer is a home cook, photographer, and writer of the food blog *Fresh Tart,* found at FreshTart.net. She also is the organizer of Minnesota Food Bloggers. Of this Asian-inflected recipe, she says, "This is the first braise I make each fall when the weather turns cold in Minnesota. It bridges the seasons so nicely, when there are still onions, garlic, peppers, scallions, and basil at the farmers' markets, but everyone is hungry for something with more substance."

3 LB GRASS-FED BEEF CHUCK ROAST, CUT INTO 6 PIECES AND TRIMMED OF EXCESS FAT
COARSE SALT
1 TBSP NEUTRAL OIL
1 SMALL ONION, SLICED LENGTHWISE INTO 1-INCH PIECES
2 CLOVES GARLIC, MINCED
1 TBSP GRATED FRESH GINGER
GRATED ZEST AND JUICE (ABOUT 2 TBSP) OF 1 LIME
2 TBSP THAI GREEN CURRY PASTE

1 (13½-OZ) CAN COCONUT MILK
2 TBSP LIGHT BROWN SUGAR, PLUS MORE TO TASTE
2 TBSP THAI FISH SAUCE, PLUS MORE TO TASTE
1 GREEN BELL PEPPER, SEEDED, DERIBBED, AND CUT INTO 1-INCH PIECES
2 SCALLIONS, CHOPPED
¼ CUP THINLY SLICED FRESH BASIL
COOKED RICE, FOR SERVING

Serves 6

1 Preheat the oven to 275°F.

2 Sprinkle the beef pieces with coarse salt.

3 Heat the oil in a Dutch oven over medium-high heat until shimmering. Working in batches, add 2–3 pieces of beef at a time and brown thoroughly; it should take no less than 15 minutes. Transfer the beef to a plate as you work.

4 When all the beef is browned, reduce the heat to medium and add the onion, garlic, ginger, lime zest, and curry paste to the pot. Cook, stirring, for 2–3 minutes. Stir in the coconut milk, brown sugar, and fish sauce.

5 Return the beef pieces to the pot with any accumulated juices from the plate and bring to a simmer. Cover tightly and transfer the pot to the oven. Bake until the beef is fork-tender, 2–3 hours. Remove the beef pieces to a cutting board.

6 Set the pot over medium heat, and when the sauce simmers, stir in the bell pepper and simmer uncovered for a few minutes until tender. Stir in the lime juice and taste for seasoning; add more fish sauce for saltiness, more sugar for sweetness, more lime for sourness.

7 Stir in the scallions and basil. Pull the beef into bite-size pieces and return to the pan. Stir the beef into the sauce and serve immediately with hot rice.

KRISTIN TOMBERS

Meat matters

Clancey's Meats and Fish, in the Linden Hills neighborhood of South Minneapolis, is a carnivore's cache packed with foie gras, herb-scented pâtés, house-cured meats, jewel-toned chutneys, relishes, and, of course, thick cuts of pastured beef, pork, and poultry, pearly scallops, and pink-veined shrimp, ready to wrap in thick butcher paper.

Stock up on house-made stock (chicken, veal, lamb, and fish fumet) and find that odd cut such as lamb heart or hog liver. Everything comes from nearby farms—Hill and Vale, Hidden Stream, Au Bon Canard, and Pat Ebnet's Wild Acres, as well as Coastal Seafoods. Owner Kristin Tombers buys whole animals to butcher in-house. Everything is used, nothing wasted, except, perhaps, the squeal.

Linden Hill Meats looks pretty much the same since Tombers took over from LeRoy Draeger. It's a shoebox of a space, its cases piled high with coils of sausages and slabs of meat of varying thickness. What is missing, though, is the smell. There's no acrid scent of old blood or nose-singeing cleaning fluids. This place is as fresh as a sunny grass field.

It's because Clancey's meat is from pasture-raised animals, mostly butch-ered in-house. Tombers explains, "In my opinion, when animals are raised industrially, in confinement, on chemi-cally treated feed, their meat has an off flavor, and if that meat is kept in Cryovac packs so that the blood pools up, it can smell rank." She says, "I have not experienced that awful stench with pasture-raised animals." There is also a big difference in flavor between pas-tured meat and commodity meat, she continues. "The meat from animals that have been outside, feeding on pasture, is leaner and cleaner tasting than indus-trially produced commodity meat."

Clancey's sausages are shining examples of Tombers' knowledge and skill. The tiny kitchen makes between 120 and 150 pounds per week, chang-ing its selections through the seasons. They've created thirty different reci-pes, each uncommon. Consider citrus marmalade duck sausage with meat from Caledonia; Minnesota's Au Bon Canard foie gras ducks; blueberry lamb sausage, inspired by a friend's grilled lamb dish with blueberry coulis; or a simple breakfast sausage with hints of vanilla. Come the holidays, you won't want to miss the fig and chestnut pork sausage, and in July, find fennel pollen bratwurst with a light licorice scent, made to grill.

Clancey's fine meats are packaged with care and comforting culinary advice. No matter how crowded with customers—it's sometimes cheek to jowl, two deep at the counter—Tombers and her staff are never too busy to pause and listen, then proffer advice. "People really care about this food," she says. "Meat is not cheap. People who come to us have gone out of their way even though it's easier to just toss a precut package of beef or pork wrapped in plastic into their shopping cart when they're strolling down the supermarket aisle. These rela-tionships with our customers, friendships really, are important, and they just keep getting better all the time."

Tombers credits her team, a young and energetic staff of eight, for the shop's warm, welcoming vibe and its innovative offerings: marinated meats ready to grill, or sandwiches of house-made cold cuts and fresh farm veg-etables stacked on breads from Rustica Bakery. The only grind in this job is the sausage. Clancey's and its local sup-pliers are going gangbusters thanks to the interest in local, sustainable animal husbandry. Committed to her pro-ducers, staff, and customers, Kristin Tombers, of Clancey's Meats and Fish, proves that, in this vibrant community, meat matters.

BEEF FAJITAS

From Abby Andrusko, The Grass Fed Cattle Company, Edina

Beef from cows that graze out in fresh air is leaner and tastes quite different from the beef from cows raised in confinement on corn. Old-timers will tell you the meat from grass-fed cattle tastes "the way beef used to taste." The Grass Fed Cattle Company in Edina supplies the Twin Cities market with grass-fed beef from local ranchers. Because the beef is naturally leaner, it cooks quickly, so dinner comes together in a wink. In this recipe, skirt steak is sprinkled with salt and sugar to create a lovely caramelized crust that traps the juices while the steak grills. Be sure to let the meat rest before slicing; this allows those juices to redistribute so the meat remains moist and flavorful.

Edible Tip

Get your grill really, really hot immediately before cooking this steak to achieve maximum caramelization.

FOR THE SAUCE:

1 CUP MAYONNAISE
½ CUP SOUR CREAM
JUICE OF 1 LIME
HANDFUL OF FRESH CILANTRO, CHOPPED
1½ TSP CHILI POWDER
1 TSP GROUND CUMIN
PINCH OF CAYENNE PEPPER
A FEW DASHES OF YOUR FAVORITE HOT SAUCE

FOR THE FAJITAS:

2 LB SKIRT STEAK, TRIMMED OF FAT
1 TBSP OLIVE OIL
1½ TSP FRESHLY GROUND BLACK PEPPER
1½ TSP SALT
1½ TSP SUGAR
8–12 FLOUR TORTILLAS

Serves 4–6

MAKE THE SAUCE:

1 Whisk together the mayonnaise, sour cream, lime juice, cilantro, chili powder, cumin, cayenne, and hot sauce in a medium bowl. Taste and adjust the seasonings, adding more hot sauce if desired. Transfer to a serving bowl.

MAKE THE FAJITAS:

2 Rub the meat with the olive oil and season with pepper, cover with foil, and let rest for 2 hours in the refrigerator. Remove the meat from the refrigerator so that it comes to room temperature, about 1 hour.

3 Prepare a charcoal grill for high heat or preheat a gas grill to high. (Alternately, preheat a broiler to high.) Sprinkle both sides of the meat with the salt and then the sugar. Grill (or broil) so that the meat caramelizes and a crust forms, about 2 minutes. Rotate the meat 90 degrees (if grilling) and continue cooking another 2 minutes. Flip the meat and continue cooking until it is done to your likeness, 3 minutes for rare, 5 minutes for well done.

4 Set the meat on a plate to rest for 7–10 minutes before cutting across the grain and at a 45-degree angle to the cutting board into 2-inch slices. Transfer the meat slices and any juices to a serving platter.

5 Place a tortilla on a microwave-safe plate, and cover with a lightly dampened paper towel. Alternate tortillas with paper towels. Microwave on high for about 30 seconds to 1 minute to warm through. Alternately, preheat the oven to 250°F. Stack the tortillas in a dish towel and place on a plate or in a casserole of a similar size. Cover with foil or a lid. Place in the oven until warmed through, about 20 minutes.

6 Serve the tortillas, meat, and sauce and have everyone assemble their own fajitas.

SALSA VERDE BEEF STEW

*From Jennette Turner,
natural foods educator*

Jennette Turner wrote this recipe because her sister "literally had buckets of tomatillos in her garden one year and we were looking for things to do with them." Plus, Turner says, she loves Mexican food. Turner says this stew is "delicious with warmed corn tortillas or corn chips from Whole Grain Milling." (Read more about Turner on page 47.)

1 TBSP BUTTER OR OLIVE OIL
1 ONION, CHOPPED (1 CUP)
1 LB BEEF STEW CHUNKS
1 LB POTATOES, PEELED AND
    CUBED
1 MEDIUM ZUCCHINI, CHOPPED
1 LB TOMATILLOS, HUSKED,
    RINSED, AND COARSELY
    CHOPPED
1 BELL PEPPER (ANY COLOR),
    SEEDED, DERIBBED, AND
    CHOPPED

1 (4 OZ) CAN DICED GREEN CHILES
3 CUPS BEEF STOCK
1½ TSP SALT
1 TSP GROUND CUMIN
1–2 CUPS CORN, FROZEN OR CUT
    FRESH FROM THE COB
SOUR CREAM FOR SERVING
    (OPTIONAL)
½ CUP FRESH CILANTRO LEAVES,
    FOR GARNISH (OPTIONAL)

Serves 4

1 Warm the butter in a large Dutch oven. Add the onion and cook for 3–4 minutes. Add the beef and sauté until browned, 7–8 minutes.

2 Add the potatoes, zucchini, tomatillos, bell pepper, chiles, stock, salt, and cumin. Bring to a boil, reduce the heat to low, cover, and cook until the beef and vegetables are very tender, 1–2 hours.

3 Add the corn and continue cooking to heat through. Serve with sour cream and cilantro, if desired.

Edible Tips

To use and store tomatillos: Remove the papery brown husk and rinse off the sticky resin that's on the skin. Keep the tomatillos in a paper bag in the refrigerator. They will last up to a month.
   To make this stew in a slow cooker: Omit the butter or oil used to cook the onion. Put everything in a slow cooker except the corn. Mix well. Cook on low for 6–8 hours. Add the corn and continue cooking until heated through.

VENISON LOIN IN PANCETTA WITH CRANBERRIES

*From Beth Dooley,
Minneapolis food writer*

Venison is deer meat, and Minnesota cooks have developed a stunning variety of ways to cook it: venison steaks, venison meatloaf, burgers, stew, and so on. The loin, or backstrap, is the most prized cut of venison, says Beth Dooley. The loin is lean, though flavorful, Dooley says, and works nicely as a substitute in recipes calling for pork loin. Here cranberries make a sweet-tart accent to the savory meat.

Edible Fact

Venison is popular in Minnesota because deer hunting is so popular. Last year, nearly five hundred thousand hunters participated in the firearms deer season, reports Minnesota's Department of Natural Resources (DNR). About 30 percent of those hunters were successful. According to the DNR, Minnesota's whitetail deer population totals about 1 million.

¼ TSP COARSE SALT
¼ TSP FRESHLY GROUND BLACK PEPPER
¼ CUP CHOPPED FRESH THYME
1½ LB VENISON, SILVER SKIN REMOVED
8 OZ PANCETTA, CUT INTO STRIPS
2 TBSP VEGETABLE OIL
2 TBSP UNSALTED BUTTER
1 SHALLOT, COARSELY CHOPPED
¼ CUP ORANGE JUICE
½ CUP FRESH CRANBERRIES
1 TBSP HONEY

Serves 4

1 Preheat the oven to 350°F.

2 Mix together the salt, pepper, and thyme in a small bowl and rub into the venison.

3 Heat the oil in a large skillet over medium-high heat. Add the venison and brown on all sides. Transfer to a baking dish. (Reserve the skillet.) When the venison is cool enough to handle wrap the pancetta strips around the middle and ends of the meat and secure with toothpicks.

4 Roast the meat until the internal temperature registers 135°F on an instant-read thermometer, 7–8 minutes. Remove the meat from the oven to let rest while you make the sauce.

5 Return the skillet to the stove and melt the butter over medium heat. Add the shallot and cook until it begins to brown, about 2 minutes. Add the orange juice and cranberries and cook until the cranberries begin to pop, 3–5 minutes. Stir in the honey.

6 Slice the meat into ½-inch slices and arrange on a serving platter or individual plates. Drizzle some of the cranberry sauce over the meat and pass the rest of it.

BLUE CHEESE AND APPLE PORK CHOPS

*From Jennette Turner,
natural foods educator*

These pork chops would go well with mashed potatoes and boiled kale, says Jennette Turner. She has been educating people about the benefits of choosing natural foods to achieve better health for nearly fifteen years. Turner teaches throughout Minneapolis and St. Paul at various venues, including several of the Twin Cities–area food co-ops.

EXTRA-VIRGIN OLIVE OIL
4 (5 OZ) BONELESS PORK SIRLOIN
  CHOPS
SALT
1 LARGE APPLE, PEELED, CORED,
  AND DICED
1 TSP RUBBED SAGE

3 OZ BLUE CHEESE, CRUMBLED
¼ CUP COARSELY CHOPPED
  WALNUTS
BABY SPINACH, FOR SERVING
  (OPTIONAL)

Serves 4

1 Preheat the broiler to high. Lightly grease a broiling pan with olive oil.

2 Place the chops in the pan, sprinkle with salt, and broil for 5–6 minutes.

3 Meanwhile, mix together the apple, sage, blue cheese, and walnuts.

4 Turn the chops over and broil until almost done, 4 minutes. Spread the apple mixture over the chops and broil for 2 minutes. Serve on a bed of spinach or other greens if desired.

Edible Nutrition Tip

Recipe author Jennette Turner says pork is a great source of vitamin B_6, or pyridoxine, a nutrient critical for the metabolism of stored carbohydrates and energy regulation.

MIDWINTER GARLICKY LAMB STEW

From Lucia Watson, chef and owner of Lucia's Restaurant, Lucia's Wine Bar, and Lucia's to Go

Stew is very popular in Minnesota because, well, it gets very cold up here. And while beef stew tends to be the most popular, the slightly sweeter, gamier lamb stew is just as delicious and is a favorite of Lucia Watson. (Read more about Watson on page 11.)

4 LB BONELESS LAMB SHOULDER, CUBED
8 CLOVES GARLIC, SLIVERED
3 SPRIGS FRESH ROSEMARY
1 CARROT, DICED, PLUS ONE CARROT CUT INTO 1-INCH PIECES
1 STALK CELERY, DICED
1 RED BELL PEPPER, SEEDED, DERIBBED, AND DICED
1 MEDIUM ONION, DICED
3 TBSP COARSELY CHOPPED FRESH PARSLEY LEAVES

3 TBSP EXTRA-VIRGIN OLIVE OIL
1 CUP FRUITY RED WINE, SUCH AS MALBEC
4 CUPS CANNED CRUSHED TOMATOES
3–4 CUPS BEEF STOCK
3 SAGE LEAVES, CHOPPED
COOKED RICE, NOODLES, OR SOFT POLENTA, FOR SERVING

Serves 6

1 Toss together the lamb, garlic, and rosemary in a large bowl; cover with plastic wrap and set aside at room temperature.

2 Combine the diced carrot, celery, bell pepper, onion, and parsley in a food processor and pulse together until coarsely chopped.

3 Warm the oil in a large Dutch oven over medium-high heat until it ripples. Add the vegetable mixture and cook until lightly browned, 8–10 minutes. Working in batches if necessary, add the lamb and fry gently in the vegetable mixture until browned on all sides.

4 Add the carrot pieces, red wine and crushed tomatoes and increase the heat to medium-high. Pour in enough stock to just barely cover the meat. Add the sage to the pot, stir well to combine, and cook over medium heat, uncovered, until the meat is almost falling-apart tender, about 2 hours. Transfer the meat to a bowl and continue to cook down the sauce until it thickens and turns glossy.

5 Ladle spoonfuls of the meat over rice, noodles, or soft polenta, and drizzle with the sauce.

SAVORY SPICY TURKEY TENDERLOINS

From Jane Peterson. assistant manager of Ferndale Market

Ask a Minnesota turkey farmer for a recipe, and of course they'll send you one for turkey tenderloins. Imagine that. This recipe comes from Jane Peterson, assistant manager of Cannon Falls–based Ferndale Market, whose owners, including Peterson, are both turkey farmers and shopkeepers—and that's turkeys as in free-range turkeys. The folks at Ferndale are committed to sustainability and local foods. Beyond their own products, they carry goods from more than sixty area food producers.

2 CLOVES GARLIC, MINCED
2 TBSP EXTRA-VIRGIN OLIVE OIL
1 TBSP LIGHT BROWN SUGAR
1 TBSP COARSE SALT
1 TSP HOT PAPRIKA
PINCH OF CAYENNE PEPPER
PINCH OF FRESHLY GROUND
   BLACK PEPPER

1½–2 LB TURKEY BREAST
   TENDERLOINS
WARM ROLLS OR SALAD GREENS,
   FOR SERVING

Serves 6–8

1 Combine the garlic, oil, brown sugar, salt, paprika, cayenne, and black pepper in a small bowl. Massage the spice paste into the turkey tenderloins. Place them in a resealable plastic bag and refrigerate for 1 hour. Remove from the refrigerator, place on a platter, loosely tent with foil, and let come to room temperature.

2 Preheat a gas grill to medium. Grill the tenderloins, turning, until the internal temperature of the thickest part of the meat registers 165°F on an instant-read thermometer, about 8 minutes per side. Transfer to a clean platter, tent with foil, and let rest for 10 minutes.

3 Slice the tenderloins thickly, on the bias, and serve on warm rolls or atop fresh salad greens.

BUTTERNUT SQUASH LASAGNA

*From Elizabeth Ries,
co-host of* Twin Cities Live
on KSTP-TV Channel 5

Elizabeth Ries planted butternut squash in her garden in Minneapolis this year and harvested eight of them by the end of summer. "This is my favorite way to use butternut squash. It's creamy but light at the same time. Even people who say they don't like squash will love this lasagna."

1 TBSP OLIVE OIL
1 (2½ LB) BUTTERNUT SQUASH, PEELED, SEEDED, AND DICED
SALT
FRESHLY GROUND BLACK PEPPER
½ STICK (4 TBSP) UNSALTED BUTTER
¼ CUP ALL-PURPOSE FLOUR
3½ CUPS MILK
⅛ TSP FRESHLY GRATED NUTMEG
⅛ TSP GROUND CINNAMON

½ CUP LIGHTLY PACKED FRESH BASIL LEAVES
2½ CUPS SHREDDED WHOLE-MILK MOZZARELLA CHEESE
1 (8 OZ) BOX FLAT-EDGED OVEN-READY (NO-BOIL) LASAGNA NOODLES
⅓ CUP GRATED PARMESAN CHEESE

Serves 8–10

1 Preheat the oven to 350°F. Lightly coat a 13 x 9-inch baking pan with cooking spray.

2 Heat the olive oil in a large skillet over medium-high heat. Add the squash and toss to coat. Add ½ cup water, reduce the heat to a simmer, cover, and cook until tender, about 20 minutes. Cool slightly. Puree the squash in a food processor and season with salt and pepper to taste.

3 Melt the butter in a medium saucepan over medium heat. Add the flour, whisking for 1 minute. Increase the heat to high and gradually whisk in the milk. Bring to a boil. Reduce to a simmer and cook until slightly thickened, about 5 minutes. Whisk in the nutmeg and cinnamon. Let cool slightly. Pour half the white sauce into a blender, add the basil, and blend until smooth.

4 Return the basil sauce to the saucepan and combine with the rest of the white sauce. Season with salt and pepper to taste.

5 Reserve 1 cup of the mozzarella. Make 3 layers in the prepared baking pan in this order: ¾ cup of the basil sauce, 3 noodles (placed crosswise), one-third of the squash puree, ½ cup mozzarella. Make a final layer of 3 noodles, the remaining sauce, and the reserved cup of mozzarella and Parmesan.

6 Cover with foil and bake for 40 minutes. Remove the foil and bake for 15 minutes more.

7 Let stand for 10 minutes before cutting.

GRILLED COUNTRY CHICKEN AND LIGHT BARBECUE MARINADE

From Jeanne Reiland, Edible Twin Cities *sales representative*

Like most midwestern and western states, Minnesota has welcomed its share of new residents over the years who have come from other states, and who bring along family recipes. Jeanne Reiland, originally from upstate New York, is a case in point. Now a member of the *Edible Twin Cities* staff, she's proud to share her barbecue marinade recipe, which has been "passed down from my grandmother to my mother to me and now my children. It is a lighter sauce and produces a nicely browned and moist chicken. I have found the chicken is much moister if cooked in halves. The chickens can flare up, so watch the grill carefully." This recipe makes more than enough for a church picnic or supper, a benefit, or a get-together involving a lot of hungry people; the leftovers freeze beautifully for up to 4 months.

1 CUP VEGETABLE OIL
2 CUPS CIDER VINEGAR
1 LARGE EGG
3 TBSP SALT
1 TBSP POULTRY SEASONING
¼ TSP FRESHLY GROUND WHITE PEPPER
8 (4 LB) CHICKENS, SPLIT IN HALF

Serves 16 hungry or 24 average people

1 Combine the oil, vinegar, egg, salt, poultry seasoning, and pepper in a blender and process until smooth.

2 Divide the marinade among 4–6 gallon-size resealable plastic bags. Add 3–4 chicken halves to each bag. Seal the bags and massage the marinade into the chicken. Refrigerate for up to 2 hours.

3 Preheat a gas grill to medium high heat. Remove the chickens from the marinade and grill skin-side down over indirect heat, basting them frequently with the marinade and flipping them over, until the skin has darkened and the thickest part of the thigh registers 165°F on an instant-read thermometer, 15–20 minutes per side. As the chicken halves are done, transfer them to a large platter and tent with foil. (Discard any remaining marinade.)

4 Serve with an enormous stack of napkins.

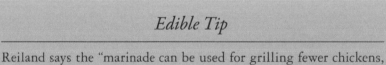

Edible Tip

Reiland says the "marinade can be used for grilling fewer chickens, perhaps one or two chickens, or five pounds of wings."

MAPLE-RHUBARB BRAISED BEEF

*From Beth Fisher, chef
of Wise Acre Eatery*

Wise Acre Eatery's farm-to-table fare has taken Minneapolis by storm since the restaurant opened its doors in the summer of 2011. The restaurant is a natural extension of what the owners, Scott Endres and Dean Engelmann, have already developed. The two own Tangletown Gardens on Fifty-Fourth and Nicollet Avenue South, a thriving urban garden center in Minneapolis. In fact, Wise Acre is just across the street from Tangletown. Plus, they own a 130-acre farm just west of the Twin Cities with rich resources, including an established community-supported agriculture (CSA) program and animals, such as chickens, hogs, and Scottish Highland cattle. Wise Acre Eatery's straight-from-the-farm menu has been a big hit. This recipe is from the restaurant's chef, Beth Fisher. *Note:* The meat needs to be marinated a day prior to cooking.

FOR THE DRY RUB:
½ CUP KOSHER SALT
⅛ CUP FRESHLY GROUND BLACK PEPPER
3 TSP GROUND ALLSPICE

FOR THE BEEF:
4-LB GRASS-FED BEEF CHUCK ROAST
1 STICK (8 TBSP) UNSALTED BUTTER
4 CUPS DICED YELLOW ONIONS
8–10 CLOVES GARLIC, PEELED

1 (4-INCH) PIECE FRESH GINGER, PEELED AND SLICED INTO ROUNDS
6 BAY LEAVES
12 SPRIGS FRESH THYME
2 CUPS DRY WHITE WINE
1 CUP MAPLE SYRUP
4–6 CUPS CHICKEN STOCK
2 LB RHUBARB, FRESH OR FROZEN, CHOPPED
2 TBSP BLACK PEPPERCORNS

Serves 6

MAKE THE DRY RUB:

1 Combine the salt, pepper, and allspice.

PREPARE THE BEEF:

2 One day prior to preparing the braised beef, rub the dry rub all over the beef, cover, and refrigerate.

3 Preheat the oven to 325°F.

4 Melt the butter in a large Dutch oven over medium-high heat. When the foam subsides, add the meat and sear on all sides, until well browned, 10–15 minutes. Transfer the meat to a platter.

5 Add the onions, garlic to taste, ginger, bay leaves, and thyme to the pan. Stir well and cook until the mixture begins to grow aromatic, about 5 minutes.

6 Return the roast to the pan and add the wine, maple syrup, and just enough chicken stock to come three-quarters of the way up the sides of the roast. Increase the heat to high, add the rhubarb and peppercorns, bring to a boil, and cook for 5 minutes.

7 Cover and place in the oven to roast for 2 hours. Remove the pan from the oven and let the roast rest in the braising liquid for 20 minutes.

8 Slice the meat thinly and cover loosely with foil. Strain the braising liquid into a medium saucepan and discard the solids. Reheat, tasting for seasoning. Spoon the sauce over the meat before serving.

LAAB MOO AND KHAO NEOW (SAVORY CHOPPED PORK SALAD WITH STEAMED STICKY RICE)

From Joe Hatch-Surisook, chef and owner of Sen Yai Sen Lek, Minneapolis

Joe Hatch-Surisook's culinary experience started in his family's kitchens in Bangkok and continued later in Chicago. He says he learned traditional techniques and "careful balancing of flavors," so integral to Thai cuisine, at his mother's side. In September 2008, he and his wife, Holly, opened Sen Yai Sen Lek (Big Noodle Little Noodle), their critically acclaimed Thai rice and noodles restaurant in Northeast Minneapolis. Hatch-Surisook says his goal at Sen Yai Sen Lek is to offer authentic preparations of traditional Thai comfort food using local and sustainably produced ingredients. Community involvement and family ownership round out the restaurant's guiding principles, influenced by Hatch-Surisook's personal life philosophy. Sen Yai Sen Lek has received numerous awards, including a Best New Restaurant nod from *Mpls.-St. Paul* magazine and Best Thai Restaurant from *City Pages*.

Edible Tip

Serve the pork and rice with fresh raw vegetables such as cucumber, green beans, and greens.

FOR THE RICE:
2 CUPS STICKY RICE (ALSO KNOWN AS THAI SWEET RICE)

FOR THE SALAD:
3 TBSP STICKY RICE (THAI SWEET RICE)
1½ LB PORK SHOULDER, COARSELY CHOPPED, OR COARSE GROUND PORK
¼ CUP FRESH LIME JUICE
3 TBSP FISH SAUCE
¼ CUP THINLY SLICED SHALLOTS
¼ CUP CHOPPED SCALLIONS, WHITE AND LIGHT GREEN PARTS ONLY
2 TBSP THAI CHILE POWDER
¼ CUP CHOPPED FRESH CILANTRO
¼ CUP CHOPPED FRESH MINT

Serves 4

MAKE THE RICE:

1 Rinse the rice under cold water until the water runs clear, about 30 seconds.

2 Place the rice in a bowl, cover with cold water, and soak for at least 6 hours. Alternately, soak the rice in hot tap water for 3 hours.

3 Drain the uncooked rice and place it in a steamer basket lined with cheesecloth. Cover the steamer basket and steam the rice over boiling water for 15–20 minutes. Transfer to a covered serving bowl.

MAKE THE SALAD:

4 Toast the uncooked rice in a dry skillet over medium heat until lightly browned. Grind into a powder using a coffee grinder or spice grinder.

5 Fill a medium saucepan with 2 cups of water and bring to a boil over medium-high heat. Add the pork and cook, stirring it to break it up, until just cooked through, 1–2 minutes. With a slotted spoon, transfer the pork to a large bowl.

6 Add the lime juice, fish sauce, shallots, scallions, and chile powder to the pork and toss to combine. Add the toasted rice, cilantro, and mint and gently mix again.

7 Serve the salad over the steamed sticky rice.

BLACK BEAN BURGERS

*From Elizabeth Ries,
co-host of* Twin Cities Live
on KSTP-TV Channel 5

TV host Elizabeth Ries says that she is a former vegetarian, but even "though I'm back to being an omnivore, I still adore these burgers." She acknowledges that with all its different components, this recipe might appear complicated—but all the parts "come together quickly," so it's much easier than it looks. Plus, she says, the aioli is also a great dipping sauce for sweet potato fries. Ries says she learns from chefs every day on her television show and takes home their "ideas and flavor combinations."

FOR THE CORN SALSA:
1 CUP CORN KERNELS, FRESH OR
   THAWED FROZEN
½ CUP SEEDED AND DICED TOMATO
1 SCALLION, CHOPPED
1½ TBSP CHOPPED FRESH CILANTRO
2 TSP SEEDED AND MINCED
   JALAPEÑO PEPPER
2 TSP FRESH LIME JUICE
SALT

FOR THE GUACAMOLE:
2 SMALL HASS AVOCADOS
1 TBSP FRESH LIME JUICE
SALT

FOR THE LIME-CILANTRO AIOLI:
⅓ CUP MAYONNAISE
⅓ CUP PLAIN GREEK YOGURT
   (WHOLE-MILK OR 2%)
2 TBSP FRESH LIME JUICE
½ CUP FRESH CILANTRO, CHOPPED

1 CLOVE GARLIC, CRUSHED
   THROUGH A PRESS
SALT
FRESHLY GROUND BLACK PEPPER

FOR THE BLACK BEAN BURGERS:
⅓ CUP CHOPPED ONION
2 CLOVES GARLIC, PEELED AND
   LEFT WHOLE
1 TSP GROUND CUMIN
1½ CUPS CANNED BLACK BEANS,
   DRAINED AND RINSED
½ CUP FINE, DRIED BREADCRUMBS
⅓ CUP CHOPPED FRESH CILANTRO
¾ CUP WALNUTS, TOASTED AND
   FINELY CHOPPED
KOSHER SALT
FRESHLY GROUND BLACK PEPPER
1 LARGE EGG, LIGHTLY BEATEN
4 WHOLE-GRAIN BUNS

Serves 4

MAKE THE CORN SALSA:
1 Stir together the corn, tomato, scallion, cilantro, jalapeño, and lime juice. Add salt to taste.

MAKE THE GUACAMOLE:
2 Pit the avocados and scoop the flesh into a bowl. Mash with the lime juice. Add salt to taste.

MAKE THE LIME-CILANTRO AIOLI:
3 Combine the mayonnaise, yogurt, lime juice, cilantro, garlic, and salt and black pepper to taste and blend thoroughly.

MAKE THE BLACK BEAN BURGERS:
4 Combine the onion, garlic, and cumin in a food processor and pulse until coarsely chopped but not pureed. Add the beans, breadcrumbs, and cilantro. Pulse until just combined. Transfer the mixture to a bowl, stir in the walnuts, and season with salt and pepper to taste. Fold in the egg and stir until combined.

5 Wet your hands with cold water and form into 4 patties. Transfer the patties to a plate, cover, and chill for at least 1 hour.

6 Oil and preheat a heavyweight grill pan over medium-high heat. Cook the patties until light brown and crispy, 4–6 minutes per side. While the patties are cooking, toast the buns.

7 Spread guacamole on the bottom of a bun; top with a burger and corn salsa. Spread aioli on the inside of the bun top and cover the burger. Serve hot.

FERNDALE TURKEY MEATLOAF

From Jane Peterson, assistant manager of Ferndale Market

File this under Minnesota comfort food, says Jane Peterson, assistant manager of Ferndale Market in Cannon Falls, about a half hour south of Minneapolis. Ferndale Market offers a stunning selection of sustainable and artisanal foods. Peterson's family runs the market and also continues to operate its turkey farm, which has been in the family since 1939.

1½ LB GROUND TURKEY (USE GROUND TURKEY CONTAINING AT LEAST HALF DARK MEAT)
1 LARGE EGG
¼ CUP WHOLE MILK
¾ CUP FINE, DRIED BREADCRUMBS OR QUICK-COOKING OATS
½ CUP CHOPPED ONION
2 TBSP CHOPPED GREEN BELL PEPPER

2 TSP MINCED GARLIC (OPTIONAL)
1 TSP ITALIAN HERB SEASONING
1 TSP SALT
¼ TSP FRESHLY GROUND BLACK PEPPER
¼ CUP KETCHUP
2 TBSP LIGHT BROWN SUGAR

Serves 6

1 Preheat the oven to 350°F.

2 Combine the turkey, egg, milk, breadcrumbs, onion, bell pepper, garlic (if using), Italian seasoning, salt, and black pepper in a large bowl. Place the mixture in a nonstick or glass 9 x 5-inch loaf pan and bake for 45 minutes.

3 Meanwhile, stir together the ketchup and brown sugar in a small bowl.

4 Remove the meatloaf from the oven, and using an icing spatula, spread the ketchup mixture over the top. Return the meatloaf to the oven and bake about 15 minutes more, or until the meat is firm, the juices run clear, and an instant-read thermometer registers at least 160°F when inserted at least 1 inch from edge of pan.

5 Let stand for 10 minutes before serving.

MAHI-MAHI FISH TACOS WITH MANGO SALSA AND COLESLAW

*From Paulette Mitchell,
cookbook author, food writer,
and television personality*

Local residents will think of this one as a brief tropical vacation—via food. Although they are not grown locally, beautiful fresh mangoes are available at the Minneapolis Farmers Market during the summer. Their juiciness and fresh flavor are welcome on a hot summer day, especially when paired with other tasty ingredients to make a mouthwatering salsa. This recipe calls for mahi-mahi, a fish found in much warmer climates, but can also be prepared with another firm white fish, such as orange roughy, grouper, or snapper. Mitchell's most recent cookbook is *The Complete 15-Minute Gourmet: Creative Cuisine Made Fast and Fresh*.

FOR THE MANGO SALSA:
½ TSP GRATED LIME ZEST
2 TBSP FRESH LIME JUICE
1 TBSP EXTRA-VIRGIN OLIVE OIL
1 TSP FINELY CHOPPED FRESH
  GINGER
⅛ TSP CAYENNE PEPPER
2 CUPS MANGO (¼-INCH) CUBES
½ RED BELL PEPPER, FINELY
  CHOPPED
¼ CUP FINELY CHOPPED SHALLOTS
2 TBSP FINELY CHOPPED FRESH
  CILANTRO
SALT
COARSELY GROUND BLACK PEPPER

FOR THE COLESLAW:
½ CUP MAYONNAISE
1 TBSP FRESH LIME JUICE
¼ MEDIUM HEAD GREEN CABBAGE,
  SHREDDED
2 SCALLIONS, THINLY SLICED

2 TBSP FINELY CHOPPED FRESH
  CILANTRO
DASH OF SALT AND PEPPER

FOR THE FISH:
¾ LB MAHI-MAHI
1 CLOVE GARLIC, MINCED
1 TSP CHILI POWDER
½ TSP GROUND CORIANDER
¼ TSP GROUND CUMIN
¼ TSP PAPRIKA
VEGETABLE OIL

FOR THE TACOS:
1 AVOCADO, CUT INTO ¼-INCH DICE
JUICE OF 1 LIME
½ CUP SOUR CREAM OR PLAIN
  YOGURT
8 (7-INCH) FLOUR TORTILLAS

Serves 4

MAKE THE MANGO SALSA:

1 Stir together the lime zest, lime juice, oil, ginger, and cayenne in a medium bowl. Add the mango, bell pepper, shallots, and cilantro and stir until evenly combined. Season with salt and pepper to taste.

MAKE THE COLESLAW:

2 Combine the mayonnaise and lime juice in a medium bowl. Add the cabbage, scallions, cilantro, and salt and pepper and stir to combine.

MAKE THE FISH:

3 Pat the fish dry. Stir together the garlic, chili powder, coriander, cumin, and paprika in a small bowl. Brush both sides of the fish with oil and then rub evenly with the spices. (The fish can be covered and chilled for up to 1 hour before grilling.)

4 Preheat a gas grill or grill pan. Cook the fish until opaque and flaky, 3–5 minutes per side. Cut into 1-inch strips.

PREPARE THE TACOS:

5 Just before serving, stir together the avocado and lime juice in a small bowl. Spoon the sour cream into a small bowl. On the serving table, arrange separate bowls of salsa, coleslaw, avocado, and sour cream, and the fish. Place the stack of tortillas between 2 damp heavyweight paper towels and microwave on high for about 1 minute, or until warm and pliable. Instruct guests to stuff the tortillas as they wish with the filling ingredients. Roll and enjoy.

MINNESOTA HARVEST SALAD WITH CHICKEN

From Eric Simpson, executive chef of Hazeltine National Golf Club

Hazeltine National Golf Club in Chaska is well-known for having hosted a number of world-class golf events over the years. In 2009 Hazeltine hosted the PGA Championship and in 2016 will host the Ryder Cup. Beyond golf, the facility has also gained a respected reputation for the food it serves at all of its tournaments, wedding receptions, and other special events. *Note:* The chicken has to marinate overnight.

FOR THE CHICKEN:
½ CUP HONEY
½ CUP DIJON MUSTARD
1 CUP CHICKEN STOCK
½ CUP SEA SALT
4 (6 OZ) SKINLESS, BONELESS
    CHICKEN BREASTS

FOR THE SALAD:
12 OZ BABY SPINACH

12 OZ CHOPPED ROMAINE LETTUCE
4 HONEYGOLD APPLES, SLICED
1 CUP DRIED CRANBERRIES
1 CUP GOLDEN RAISINS
APPLE CIDER VINAIGRETTE
    (PAGE 108)
½ CUP HULLED PUMPKIN SEEDS
    (PEPITAS)

Serves 4

MAKE THE CHICKEN:

1 Combine the honey, mustard, stock, and salt in a large bowl. Add the chicken, cover, and marinate in the refrigerator overnight.

2 Preheat a gas grill to medium-high heat. Remove the chicken from the brine, and grill until the thickest part of the meat registers 165°F on an instant-read thermometer, about 8 minutes per side. Transfer to a platter, tent loosely with foil, and let rest for 8 minutes. Slice each chicken breast on the bias.

MAKE THE SALAD:

3 Combine the spinach, romaine, sliced apples, cranberries, and raisins in a large salad bowl. Add enough Apple Cider Vinaigrette to lightly coat the greens. Arrange the salad on a platter. Top with the sliced chicken and sprinkle with the pumpkin seeds.

APPLE CIDER VINAIGRETTE

From Eric Simpson, executive chef of Hazeltine National Golf Club

Although this recipe is part of chef Simpson's Minnesota Harvest Salad on page 107, it is a natural on any green salad where you'd like a punch of apple flavor. Once you've tried it, you'll be looking for other ways to use it.

1 CUP APPLE CIDER
1 HONEYCRISP APPLE, PEELED, CORED, AND CHOPPED
½ CUP CIDER VINEGAR
1 TBSP GRAINY MUSTARD
1 TBSP HONEY
¼ CUP CANOLA OIL
¼ CUP OLIVE OIL
SALT
FRESHLY GROUND BLACK PEPPER
CHOPPED PARSLEY

Makes about 2 cups

1 In a small saucepan, reduce the cider by half to get ½ cup.

2 Place the apple in a food processor. With the machine running, drizzle in the vinegar, mustard, honey, and reduced cider and puree until smooth. With the machine running, add the oils in a steady stream and process until the mixture emulsifies. Season with salt and pepper to taste. Add parsley to taste.

PIE PUMPKIN-BARLEY RISOTTO

From Lenny Russo,
Heartland Restaurant

This dish may be served as an accompaniment for meat or fish or may be served as a vegetarian entrée garnished with a drizzle of pumpkin seed oil and topped with some deep-fried julienned leeks or chopped toasted hazelnuts. (Read more about Russo on page 111.)

4 CUPS VEGETABLE STOCK
3 TBSP UNSALTED BUTTER
1 TBSP GRAPESEED OIL
1 WHITE ONION, CUT INTO
⅛-INCH DICE
1 CARROT, CUT INTO ⅛-INCH DICE
2 STALKS CELERY, CUT INTO
⅛-INCH DICE
1 FENNEL BULB, CORED AND CUT
INTO ⅛-INCH DICE
1 CLOVE GARLIC, MINCED
8 OZ HULLED BARLEY

1 TSP FINE SEA SALT
½ TSP FRESHLY GROUND BLACK
PEPPER
2 CUPS ROASTED PIE PUMPKIN
(PAGE 110)
¼ TSP FRESHLY GRATED NUTMEG
¼ TSP GRATED FRESH GINGER
⅛ TSP GROUND CINNAMON
1 TBSP FRESH THYME LEAVES

Serves 6 as a main course

1 Bring the stock to a slow simmer in a nonreactive pot.

2 Meanwhile, melt 1 tablespoon of the butter in the oil in a Dutch oven over medium-low heat. Add the onion, carrot, celery, fennel, and garlic and lightly sauté until tender, 5–10 minutes. Add the barley, salt, and pepper, and cook, stirring occasionally, until the mixture becomes glossy and begins to thicken.

3 Once the barley is pearlized, slowly add the stock using a 4-ounce ladle. Continue to stir the barley as you add the stock. Allow the stock to become completely absorbed before adding another ladle's worth. Repeat this process until all but 1 cup of the stock is used. The barley should be tender; it will take 45–50 minutes total.

4 Stir in the pumpkin, nutmeg, ginger, and cinnamon. Ladle in the reserved 1 cup stock and continue to stir gently. Simmer until the stock is absorbed and the pumpkin is warmed through. Remove the pan from the heat and stir in the thyme. Gently stir in the remaining 2 tablespoons butter. Taste and adjust for salt and pepper if necessary.

ROASTED PIE PUMPKIN

From Lenny Russo,
Heartland Restaurant

Pie pumpkins are smaller than the familiar Jack O' lantern and much sweeter. They roast up beautifully to use in soup, risotto or, of course, pie, says Lenny Russo.

Edible Tips

Roast several pumpkins at once and freeze the additional flesh to use in soups, breads, cookies, and pies.

You can substitute winter squash for the pie pumpkin, but it is not as sweet.

1 MEDIUM PIE PUMPKIN, ABOUT
  3½ TO 4 POUNDS
1 CUP GRAPE SEED OIL
½ TEASPOON FINE SEA SALT
¼ TEASPOON BLACK PEPPER,
  FRESHLY GROUND
⅛ TEASPOON NUTMEG, FRESHLY
  GROUND
⅛ TEASPOON GROUND GINGER
⅛ TEASPOON GROUND CINNAMON

Makes 3 cups

1 Preheat the oven to 400°F.

2 Cut the pumpkin in half lengthwise, and scoop out the seeds. Rub the flesh with the oil and the spices, and place it, flesh side down, on a sheet pan. Roast the pumpkin until the skin blisters and the pumpkin is tender, about 30 to 35 minutes.

3 Remove the pumpkin from the oven and allow it to cool. Scoop out the flesh and discard the skin. Reserve until needed for pumpkin soup.

LENNY RUSSO

Celebrating midwestern bounty

How fitting it is that chef Lenny Russo, of Heartland Restaurant & Farm Direct Market in St. Paul, makes his own prosciutto. The process relies on tradition, attention, patience, and knowledge of chemistry, magic, and wit. Bold, lush, and nuanced, prosciutto embodies the essence of its maker and its place. To say that Heartland Restaurant is a local-foods establishment is kind of like calling prosciutto Italian ham; both defy such reductive descriptions.

Russo has been a local foods pioneer for more than thirty years, doggedly seeking the region's best meats, cheeses, produce, grains, game, poultry, fish, spirits, and brews, celebrating midwestern bounty with Hoboken chutzpah and gastronomic aplomb. Heartland Restaurant & Farm Direct Market is the culmination of Russo's thirty years here, serving as executive chef for W.A. Frost & Company, St. Paul, and corporate chef of U.S. Restaurants, Aveda Corporation, and others. He managed Blackberry Creek Market, captained the famed New French Café, and opened the restaurants in the new Guthrie Theater, Minneapolis. In October of 2002, he and his wife and partner, Mega Hoehn, opened the first Heartland: A Contemporary Midwest-

ern Restaurant, a gem in the quaint Macalester-Groveland St. Paul neighborhood. When they relocated to the current grand redbrick warehouse overlooking the historic St. Paul Farmers' Market, their carefully tended, well-cured vision came to life.

Here, this rough kid from "the wrong side of Jersey" brings memories of long, loud family dinners to his broad ambitious menu. Everything is sourced from the region's farmers, cheese makers, fishmongers, cattlemen, hog farmers, and foragers, all of them friends.

Russo did not intend to become a chef when, to augment his college tuition fund, he cooked through some of Florida's best restaurants. Studying to become a clinical psychologist, he worked in hospitals both before and after leaving school. He researched and wrote extensively about the role of food in mental health, its connection to wellness and community. When he decided to make the switch to cooking full-time, his mother said, "That's not a real job." No, it was his life.

Nominated by the James Beard Foundation for Best Chef Midwest in 2010 and 2011, and named the best new restaurant by *Minnesota Monthly*, 2010, Heartland spins a menu that is as elegant as it is wild. In Heart-

land's intimate bar, nosh on plump, juice-splitting house-made sausages of venison and boar, agnolotti pasta with chanterelle mushrooms and local camembert, a hearty salad of earthy chickpeas and baby sweet potatoes. The dining room serves up two thoughtful prix fixe selections, "flora" (vegetarian) and "fauna" (meat and fish), plus à la carte options of succulent lake trout, hearty barley risotto, and thick juicy chops from Mangalitsa pigs, a heritage breed, raised in Taylors Falls, and the source for Lenny's prosciutto.

At Heartland Farm Direct Market, the adjacent deli, you'll find this chef's secret sauce (literally) and can stock up (literally) on fish fumet. Take home his signature pickles and condiments, pâté, sausages, and smoked fish. You can pick up fresh trout, thick pork chops, grass-fed beef, cured meat, and headcheese, crafted in-house. (There's a butchering area, with windows, where you can also observe this being made.) "The Heartland Farm Direct Market acts as a larder for the restaurant, and the restaurant is a facility to create value-added product for the market," Russo says. "It's a constant exchange of labor." While every chef worth his or her toque is attuned to "local," Russo's efforts are wholehearted and grand.

SNOWY WINTER LENTIL STEW

From Kelli Billstein, local writer

Kelli Billstein is a born-and-raised Minnesotan who enjoys passing the colder months with a hot cup of soup in hand. As a writer, she takes particular pleasure in writing about food. When she's not writing or cooking, Billstein can be found exploring the Twin Cities' arts and restaurant scenes.

1½ TBSP OLIVE OIL
1 CUP CHOPPED ONION
3 CLOVES GARLIC, MINCED
5 CUPS CHICKEN OR VEGETABLE
  STOCK
1 CUP LENTILS, RINSED AND
  PICKED OVER
½ CUP CHOPPED CARROT
2 BAY LEAVES
3 CUPS SPINACH LEAVES
1½ CUPS PEELED, CUBED WAXY
  (BOILING) POTATOES

1 CAN (14½ OZ) DICED TOMATOES,
  DRAINED
1 TSP DRIED BASIL
1 TSP DRIED SAGE
½ TSP DRIED THYME
½ TSP FRESHLY GROUND BLACK
  PEPPER
3 TBSP CHOPPED FRESH PARSLEY

Serves 6

1 Heat the oil in a large pot over medium heat until shimmering. Add the onion and garlic and cook until the onions turn translucent, about 5 minutes.

2 Add the stock, lentils, carrot, and bay leaves and bring to a boil. Reduce to a simmer, partially cover, and cook for 20 minutes. Add the spinach and potatoes and bring to a boil. Reduce to a simmer and cook until the potatoes are tender, about 15 minutes.

3 Stir in the tomatoes, basil, sage, thyme, and pepper and simmer for 10 minutes. Discard the bay leaves. Garnish with the parsley and serve with a warm, thick-cut wedge of bread.

THAI-STYLE PASTA

*From Supenn Harrison, owner
of Sawatdee Thai Restaurant*

This is a curried pasta with kick, says Supenn Harrison, of Sawatdee Thai Restaurant, which has several Twin Cities locations. "Normally it rates three stars for hot but can be toned down by adding water to the sauce," says Harrison, who also is co-author, with Judy Monroe, of *Cooking the Thai Way*.

Edible Tip

If you don't use all the sauce, store any leftovers in the freezer to have ready for a quick curry kick.

FOR THE GREEN CURRY SAUCE:
1½ TBSP VEGETABLE OIL
2 TBSP THAI GREEN CURRY PASTE
1 (14 OZ) CAN COCONUT MILK
3 KAFFIR LIME LEAVES
1 STALK LEMONGRASS, TOUGH
    OUTER LEAVES REMOVED, CORE
    POUNDED AND MINCED
2 TBSP FISH SAUCE
1 FRESH CHILE, SEEDED, RIBBED,
    AND DICED
PINCH OF SUGAR

FOR THE NOODLES:
1 (8 OZ) PACKAGE RICE NOODLES
2–3 CUPS CUT-UP CARROT,
    BROCCOLI, OR CAULIFLOWER, OR
    A COMBINATION
THINLY SLICED BEEF, CHICKEN, OR
    PORK (OPTIONAL)
CILANTRO, FOR GARNISH

Serves 2

MAKE THE GREEN CURRY SAUCE:

1 Heat the oil in a wok or large skillet over medium-high heat until it shimmers. Stir in the green curry paste and cook until it softens. Pour in the coconut milk, bring to a simmer, and cook until you smell the aroma of curry, about 5 minutes. Add the Kaffir lime leaves, lemongrass, fish sauce, chile, and sugar and stir well to combine. Remove the pan from the heat, cover, and set aside.

MAKE THE NOODLES:

2 Soak the noodles as directed on the package.

3 In a vegetable steamer, steam the soaked noodles, vegetables, and meat (if using) until the vegetables are tender, about 8 minutes.

4 Divide the hot noodle mixture between 2 plates or bowls and top with as little or as much of the green curry sauce as you like. Serve hot, garnished with fresh cilantro.

PRESERVED LEMON VEGETABLE TAGINE

*From Patricia Cumbie,
advocate of cooperatives and
local organic foods*

Patricia Cumbie is the former editor of *Mix*, a publication of the Twin Cities Natural Food Co-ops. Her work as a writer and editor has taken her to many places in the United States and abroad, where she takes every opportunity to study local food and customs. Most evenings you'll find Cumbie in her kitchen, sautéing garlic and chopping herbs in preparation for a simple and delicious home-cooked meal. She says she loves this vegetable tagine recipe "because it is so versatile—it can be adapted for vegans and meat lovers alike—and makes enough if you are entertaining a group." *Note*: If you're making your own preserved lemons, they need to be started 4–6 weeks in advance. They can also be purchased at Middle Eastern grocery stores.

Of the preserved lemons, Cumbie says, "This is absolutely worth the effort. The results are ambrosial; the tangy/salty/fruity flavor of homemade preserved lemons simply cannot be duplicated with any other ingredient."

¼ CUP EXTRA-VIRGIN OLIVE OIL
1 ONION, CUT INTO CHUNKS
2 CARROTS, CUT INTO CHUNKS
8 SMALL WAXY (BOILING) POTATOES, HALVED
1 GREEN BELL PEPPER, CUT INTO CHUNKS
½ CUP GREEN BEANS, HALVED
1 TBSP GRATED FRESH GINGER
2 CLOVES GARLIC, CHOPPED
1 TSP GROUND TURMERIC
1 TBSP GROUND CORIANDER
1 TSP CUMIN SEEDS
1 TSP GROUND CINNAMON
4 CUPS VEGETABLE STOCK
2 TOMATOES, CHOPPED
¼ CUP GOLDEN RAISINS
SALT
RIND OF 1 PRESERVED LEMON, STORE-BOUGHT OR HOMEMADE (RECIPE FOLLOWS)
COOKED COUSCOUS FOR SERVING

Serves 6–8

1 Heat the oil in a large pot or tagine over medium heat until it shimmers. Add the onion, carrots, potatoes, bell pepper, and green beans, and cook until the potatoes are tender and the onions are translucent, about 10 minutes.

2 Stir in the ginger, garlic, turmeric, coriander, cumin seeds, and cinnamon, and cook for 5 minutes. Bring to a boil. Reduce the heat to medium-low and add the stock, tomatoes, and raisins. Season with salt, cover the pot, and simmer for 30 minutes. Add the preserved lemon rind and combine well. Serve on a bed of cooked couscous.

PRESERVED LEMONS

12 LEMONS, PREFERABLY MEYER
KOSHER SALT
MORE LEMONS FOR JUICING IF NEEDED

Makes 12 preserved lemons

1 Wash and dry the lemons. Quarter each lemon lengthwise, but do not cut all the way through; it should still be attached at the bottom.

2 Fill each lemon with as much salt as it will hold. Stuff the lemons into a wide-mouth glass quart jar. Compress them until there is no space left and lemon juice has risen to the top. The lemons must be covered by juice to attain a safely preserved quality. If they are not fully submerged in lemon juice, juice a few lemons to add to the juices already in the jar. Seal and set aside at room temperature for 2 weeks, then refrigerate. The lemons can be used when the rinds are tender, 4–6 weeks. Properly preserved lemons can keep in a tightly closed container for up to a year in the refrigerator.

CHAPTER 5

DESSERTS AND DRINKS

Ah, dessert. Sweet, sweet tempting dessert.

"Did you save room for dessert?" the waiter or waitress inevitably asks. "No, not tonight," you demur. "Just the check, please." Polite smiles are exchanged. Then, in the car on the way home, you think to yourself, well, actually, you did save room for dessert. You always have room for dessert. In fact, you love dessert! No worries. This chapter offers you a varied choice of dessert dishes you can make in your own kitchen. And, just for kicks and giggles, we've thrown in a few drink recipes, too. *Salut!*

LEMON-GINGER POUND CAKE

From Beth Dooley,
Minneapolis food writer

This old-fashioned cake keeps beautifully, wrapped in plastic, for several days, says Beth Dooley. Slices are also delicious toasted for breakfast or spread with ginger marmalade and served with Earl Grey tea. In addition to her work as a food journalist and cookbook author, Dooley also teaches cooking classes at the University of Minnesota Arboretum.

1 CUP ALL-PURPOSE FLOUR
⅛ TSP BAKING POWDER
1 TBSP GRATED LEMON ZEST
3 LARGE EGGS
1 CUP SUGAR
⅛ TSP SALT
¼ CUP HEAVY CREAM

1 STICK (8 TBSP) UNSALTED
   BUTTER, MELTED AND COOLED
¼ CUP CHOPPED CRYSTALLIZED
   GINGER

Makes 1 loaf

1 Preheat the oven to 325°F. Butter an 8½ x 4½-inch loaf pan. Dust with flour and tap out the excess.

2 Sift together the flour and baking powder into a medium bowl. Stir in the lemon zest. In a large bowl, using an electric mixer on high speed, beat together the eggs, sugar, and salt until thick and pale, about 2 minutes. Reduce the speed to low and slowly add the flour mixture alternating with the cream and melted butter, beginning and ending with the flour mixture and beating well after each addition. Fold in the crystallized ginger. Turn the batter into the prepared pan.

3 Bake the cake until the top is golden and a knife inserted into the center comes out clean, 60–70 minutes. Cool in the pan on a wire rack for about 15 minutes. Invert onto the rack to cool completely.

RHUBARB TART

*From Jack Gerten/Helen Gerten,
Gerten Greenhouses farm*

This tart recipe belongs to Helen Gerten, mother of St. Paul Farmers' Market manager Jack Gerten. The Gerten family raised hothouse rhubarb on their farm in Inver Grove Heights. At one point in the 1970s, they were the only greenhouse in the Midwest growing winter rhubarb, according to Jack Gerten.

FOR THE CRUST:
2 CUPS ALL-PURPOSE FLOUR
1 STICK (8 TBSP) BUTTER
¼ CUP SHORTENING
2 TBSP SUGAR

FOR THE TOPPING:
6 LARGE EGG YOLKS
2 CUPS SUGAR
¼ CUP ALL-PURPOSE FLOUR
½ TSP SALT

1 CUP EVAPORATED MILK
5 CUPS CUT-UP RHUBARB

FOR THE MERINGUE:
6 LARGE EGG WHITES
8 TBSP SUGAR
2 TSP VANILLA EXTRACT
SHREDDED COCONUT SPRINKLES

Makes 1 (9 x 13-inch) tart

MAKE THE CRUST:
1 Preheat the oven to 350°F.

2 Combine the flour, butter, shortening, and sugar until evenly mixed. Pat the mixture onto the bottom of a 9 x 13-inch baking pan. Bake until firm and set, about 10 minutes.

MAKE THE TOPPING:
3 Mix together the egg yolks, sugar, flour, salt, evaporated milk, and rhubarb, and spread over the crust mixture. Bake for 40–45 minutes.

MEANWHILE, MAKE THE MERINGUE:
4 In a large bowl, using an electric mixer, beat the egg whites to stiff peaks, adding 2 tablespoons of the sugar at a time and beating well after each addition. Beat in the vanilla.

5 Spread the meringue over the rhubarb filling. Sprinkle with coconut and return to the oven to brown, about 10 minutes.

JACK GERTEN

Farmers' market manager is link from field to table

Jack Gerten grew up with his hands in Minnesota soil. Side by side with his siblings, Gerten planted, picked, and packed white rhubarb, lettuce, celery, and tomatoes on the family's Inver Grove Heights vegetable farm. "You didn't have to worry about what you were doing after school or on the weekends," Gerten recalls. "You'd be picking tomatoes." Gerten may no longer work the soil, but he is still an integral link from field to table as manager of the state's oldest farmers' market.

Established in 1853, the St. Paul Farmers' Market pops up every Saturday in Lowertown with stall after stall of fresh vegetables, cheese, meats, bedded plants, bakery goods, honey, and more. Beyond the Saturday Lowertown market, the 145-member St. Paul Growers' Association has twenty-two markets throughout the Twin Cities metro area, some on weekdays, some on weekends, most of them seasonal.

Gerten has managed the market for fifteen years, coordinating vendors and overseeing its expansion within the suburbs. Today, the St. Paul Growers' Association maintains the market's rich tradition of selling fresh, locally grown produce directly from the grower to the consumer.

"We've kept true to our original mission," Gerten says. "We take a lot of pride in that."

Gerten's own market roots grow deep, dating back to his grandfather Frank, who in the 1920s established Gerten Greenhouses on eighty acres of Inver Grove Heights farmland. The farm passed to a second generation, Gerten's father and uncle, who raised hothouse vegetables and bedding plants. Today, Gerten's first cousins no longer sell at the market, though the family name is still present. Gerten's second cousin, Mike, sells at the market with Gerten Brothers.

Gerten has dabbled in every corner of the food industry, from grocery store management to meatpacking. He farmed and raised hogs in southern Minnesota until the 1980s farm crisis. He spent several years operating his own greenhouse retail business before taking over management of the St. Paul market.

As manager, Gerten wears many hats, says association president Vince Niemczyk. "He really has a heartfelt care about the truck gardeners [or vendors] getting a fair price and having a place to sell their produce," Niemczyk says. "[He's always looking at] what's good for the market as a whole."

While the market has grown with the times—adopting organics, adding education programming, marketing directly to consumers—Gerten marvels at how much it still resembles the place of his youth. Farm families still pick their produce by hand and haul it to market in the bed of a pickup truck in the wee-early morning hours. Growers of various nationalities—today, Hmong make up half the association's members—set up their tables in the same way the Irish, German, and Italian immigrants did years ago.

"Farming down here at the market hasn't really changed at all," Gerten says. The market's sense of community is what Gerten most appreciates. He grew up with many of the growers and watched their children grow from thigh-high rug rats to young men and women.

Many market customers are second- or third-generation shoppers, planting the seed of appreciation for fresh, local food in their own kids, Gerten says.

The St. Paul Farmers' Market is a destination, he says, a place where people meet their neighbors and growers face-to-face. It's a place that values high-quality, local food and the people who bring it to our tables.

APPLE CRANBERRY CRUMBLE PIE

From Carol J. Butler,
Wisconsin food writer

The legend of Grandmother's apple pie has lived for at least three generations in Carol Butler's family. Legend has it that Grandma's pie won the local county fair pie contest every year. Everyone wanted to know just how she did it. Well, Butler, a freelance food writer who lives in Superior, Wisconsin, says she learned her grandma's secret one day as a child and never forgot it. "To this day, my friends swear I put something extra in my pie. I don't, honest. Grandma's secret works: slice the apples very thin." Although her grandmother peeled her apples, Butler uses organic and always leaves the skin on. For a special touch, serve the pie with a dollop of fresh whipped cream.

FOR THE PIE:
1 FROZEN PIECRUST (WHOLE WHEAT CRUST WORKS VERY NICELY WITH THIS PIE), THAWED
ENOUGH APPLES TO MAKE 5–6 CUPS THINLY SLICED APPLES
2 TBSP FRESH LEMON JUICE
¼ CUP BROWN OR RAW SUGAR
2–3 TBSP ALL-PURPOSE FLOUR (ENOUGH TO LIGHTLY COAT THE APPLES)
¼ CUP FRESH CRANBERRIES
GROUND CINNAMON (OPTIONAL)

FOR THE CRUMBLE TOPPING:
⅓ CUP WHOLE WHEAT FLOUR
⅓ CUP ALL-PURPOSE FLOUR
⅓ CUP OLD-FASHIONED ROLLED OATS (NOT QUICK-COOKING)
⅔ CUP PACKED DARK BROWN SUGAR
CHOPPED WALNUTS OR PECANS (OPTIONAL)
STICK (6 TBSP) SALTED BUTTER, AT ROOM TEMPERATURE

Serves 6–8

MAKE THE PIE:

1 Preheat the oven to 350°F.

2 Press the prepared piecrust into a deep-dish pie plate. Slice the apples into a large bowl and sprinkle in the lemon juice as you go to prevent the apples from browning. Add the sugar, flour, cranberries, and cinnamon, if using, and stir to coat. Pour the filling into the pie shell.

MAKE THE CRUMBLE:

3 Combine the whole wheat flour, all-purpose flour, oats, brown sugar, and nuts, if using, in a large bowl. Use your fingertips to rub the butter into the flour mixture until you have a coarse meal with the texture of oatmeal. Carefully pour the crumble over the mound of packed apples. Press gently with your hand.

4 Transfer the pie to a baking sheet and bake until the top is golden brown and juice bubbles beneath the topping, 45–55 minutes.

5 Let rest 1 hour before slicing.

APPLE CRISP PARFAITS WITH CARAMEL SAUCE AND SPICED RUM WHIPPED CREAM

From Lisa Patrin,
food writer

The Honeycrisp apple was named Minnesota's official state fruit in 2006, and it is featured in this recipe from Lisa Patrin, who lives in Chanhassen with her husband and two boys. Patrin says she grew up in an Italian family "where the kitchen was the heart of the home."

FOR THE APPLE CRISP:
1 CUP GRANULATED SUGAR
1 CUP PLUS 1 TBSP ALL-PURPOSE FLOUR
1½ TSP GROUND CINNAMON
¾ TSP FRESHLY GRATED NUTMEG
8 HONEYCRISP APPLES, PEELED, CORED, AND SLICED
1 CUP QUICK-COOKING OATS
1 CUP PACKED LIGHT BROWN SUGAR
¼ TSP BAKING SODA
¼ TSP BAKING POWDER
1 STICK (8 TBSP) UNSALTED BUTTER, MELTED

FOR THE SPICED RUM WHIPPED CREAM:
2 CUPS HEAVY CREAM
2 TBSP CONFECTIONERS' SUGAR
1 TSP VANILLA EXTRACT
2 TBSP CAPTAIN MORGAN SPICED RUM

FOR THE PARFAITS:
1 (12¼ OZ) JAR CARAMEL SAUCE
½ CUP CHOPPED PECANS (OPTIONAL)

Makes 8 parfaits

MAKE THE APPLE CRISP:

1 Preheat the oven to 350°F. Butter a 9-inch square glass baking dish.

2 In a large bowl, whisk together the granulated sugar, 1 tablespoon of the flour, the cinnamon, and ¼ teaspoon of the nutmeg until well combined. Add the apples to the sugar mixture and toss to coat. Spread the apples in the bottom of the prepared baking dish and pour ½ cup of water over them.

3 In a separate bowl, whisk together the remaining 1 cup flour and the oats, brown sugar, baking soda, and baking powder. Stir in the melted butter. Crumble the mixture evenly over the apples. Sprinkle the remaining ½ teaspoon nutmeg over the top.

4 Bake until the top is golden brown and apples are bubbling, 40–45 minutes. Cool slightly.

MEANWHILE, MAKE THE SPICED RUM WHIPPED CREAM:

5 In a medium bowl, with an electric mixer, beat the cream, confectioners' sugar, and vanilla extract until stiff peaks form. Gently fold in the spiced rum.

MAKE THE PARFAITS:

6 Scoop some apple crisp into 8 mini-martini glasses or small wineglasses. Drizzle each with a generous spoonful of caramel sauce and top with a dollop of spiced rum whipped cream. Sprinkle with a tablespoon of chopped pecans if desired. Serve immediately.

COFFEE TOFFEE BARS WITH ALMOND GLAZE

From Kate Selner, writer of the blog Kate in the Kitchen

These tasty little bars come from local food blogger Kate Selner, whose blog can be found at KateintheKitchen.com. As Selner muses on her site, "Curious about what you get when you mix up a culinary degree with one in English composition? If you read my blog for a while, you'll surely find out. Cooking and writing are my two most treasured skills, and I love weaving them together through stories and memories. I grew up learning to cook with my mom, who patiently guided me through simple kitchen tasks and gave me the foundation to explore, learn, and grow in the kitchen."

FOR THE BARS:
2¼ CUPS SIFTED ALL-PURPOSE
    FLOUR
½ TSP BAKING POWDER
¼ TSP SALT
2 STICKS (16 TBSP) BUTTER
1 CUP PACKED LIGHT BROWN
    SUGAR
1 TSP ALMOND EXTRACT
1 TBSP INSTANT ESPRESSO POWDER

12 OZ SEMISWEET CHOCOLATE CHIPS

FOR THE GLAZE:
2 TBSP BUTTER, AT ROOM
    TEMPERATURE
1½ CUPS CONFECTIONERS' SUGAR
1 TSP ALMOND EXTRACT
1 TBSP MILK

Makes 1 (9 x 13-inch) pan

MAKE THE BARS:

1 Preheat the oven to 350°F. Coat a 9 x 13-inch baking pan with cooking spray.

2 Combine the flour, baking powder, and salt in a medium bowl. In a separate bowl, with an electric mixer, cream the butter. Add the brown sugar and cream well. Blend in the almond extract and espresso powder. Beat in the flour mixture. Then beat in the chocolate chips. Press the dough into the baking pan and bake until slightly puffed and golden brown on top, 20–25 minutes. Let cool in the pan for 10 minutes; then slice into bars and keep intact in pan.

MAKE THE GLAZE:

3 Beat together the butter, confectioners' sugar, and almond extract. Add enough milk to get a frosting of spreading consistency. Frost the bars in the pan while still warm.

COUNTRY PEAR TART

From Trotter's Café, St. Paul

What makes a sweet treat taste so much better when it's made from scratch? The extra time and care? If that's the case, knowing there are local ingredients—in this case, butter from Castle Rock Organic Farms in Osseo, Wisconsin—may make it taste even better. This recipe comes from Trotter's Café in St. Paul, where "made from scratch" is a goal achieved every day—from soup stocks, salad dressings, sauces, and salsa to whole-grain breads and desserts like this one.

FOR THE CRUST:

1 CUP UNBLEACHED ALL-PURPOSE
   FLOUR
½ TSP SALT
⅔ STICK (5⅓ TBSP) ORGANIC
   BUTTER (PREFERABLY CASTLE
   ROCK), CHILLED
2 TBSP ICE-COLD WATER

FOR THE FILLING:

¾ STICK (6 TBSP) ORGANIC BUTTER
   (PREFERABLY CASTLE ROCK)
½ CUP SUGAR
¼ CUP ALL-PURPOSE FLOUR
½ TSP FRESHLY GRATED NUTMEG
2 LARGE EGGS
1 TSP ALMOND EXTRACT
3 RIPE PEARS

Serves 8

MAKE THE CRUST:

1 Mix together the flour and salt in a medium bowl. Cut in the butter using a pastry blender or 2 knives used scissor fashion, until the particles are the size of small peas. Sprinkle with the ice water, a little at a time, tossing with a fork just until the mixture comes together. Use your hands to gather the dough into a ball. Lightly flour a pastry cloth. With a lightly floured rolling pin, roll the pastry into an 11-inch round (to fit a 9-inch tart pan). Fold the pastry into quarters and place in a 9-inch tart pan with a removable bottom, smoothing the pastry into place around the sides. Cover loosely while preparing the filling.

2 Preheat the oven to 350°F.

MEANWHILE, MAKE THE FILLING:

3 Melt the butter in small saucepan over low heat. Remove from the heat and stir in the sugar. Whisk together the flour and nutmeg in a small bowl. Whisk the flour mixture into the butter-sugar mixture. Beat in the eggs, one at a time. Stir in the almond extract. Let the custard stand while you prepare the pears.

4 Peel the pears and slice each into 8 wedges. Arrange the pears spoke-fashion in the bottom of the pastry-lined tart pan. Spoon the custard evenly over the pear wedges. Bake until golden, about 25 minutes.

BLENDER BLUEBERRY SOUP

From Ann L. Burckhardt, food writer and cookbook author

This is a tasty way to take advantage of the juicy blueberries that ripen from July through mid-August in Minnesota and Wisconsin. This particular recipe drew raves "at a TGIF party we had on our deck one summer," says Ann L. Burckhardt, who has had a long career as a food writer and editor, including twenty-four years for the Taste section of Minneapolis's *Star Tribune*. She is the author or editor of eighteen cookbooks.

3 CUPS BLUEBERRIES, PLUS MORE
   FOR GARNISH
⅓ CUP WATER OR APPLE JUICE
1 TBSP BLUEBERRY PRESERVES
   (OPTIONAL)
2 CUPS VANILLA YOGURT

¼ CUP CONFECTIONERS' SUGAR
1 CUP HALF-AND-HALF
¼ CUP WHOLE MILK

Makes 10 (½-cup) servings

1 Place the berries, water, and preserves (if using) in a blender and blend until the berries are pureed. Add the yogurt and confectioners' sugar and puree until creamy. Add the half-and-half, and puree again. Refrigerate the soup until well chilled.

2 Just before serving, puree the soup with the milk to fluff it up. Serve the soup topped with 2 or 3 fresh berries as garnish.

CRANBERRY PIE

*From Mark Ritchie, Minnesota
Secretary of State*

Pie recipes seem to be a big part of many family legacies, handed down through the generations. Desserts have staying power. This one is no exception, says Mark Ritchie, who founded the Institute for Agriculture and Trade Policy twenty-five years ago to help support threatened family farms and rural communities. He estimates that this recipe has been in his family for close to thirty years. He got it from his mother, who made this cranberry pie every year for Thanksgiving. Now, Ritchie says with a smile and a sense of pride to be carrying on a tradition, if the family is all gathering at his home for Thanksgiving, "they expect to be having this pie."

1½ CUPS FRESH OR FROZEN CRANBERRIES (FROZEN BERRIES THAWED AND DRAINED WELL)
1 (9-INCH) FROZEN PIE SHELL, THAWED
¼ CUP PACKED LIGHT BROWN SUGAR
⅓ CUP CHOPPED WALNUTS
JUICE OF 1 LEMON
½ CUP GRANULATED SUGAR
⅓ CUP MELTED BUTTER
1 LARGE EGG, BEATEN
½ CUP ALL-PURPOSE FLOUR

Serves 6–8

1 Preheat the oven to 350°F.

2 Spread the cranberries in the bottom of the pie shell.

3 Combine the brown sugar and walnuts in a small bowl. Sprinkle over the cranberries and drizzle with lemon juice.

4 In a medium bowl, using a whisk, blend together the granulated sugar and melted butter until light yellow and ribbony. Fold in the egg and the flour and combine well. Pour over the berries.

5 Bake for 45 minutes. Let cool completely on a wire rack before serving.

MARK RITCHIE

Creating a voice for sustainability

Mark Ritchie, Minnesota's secretary of state, founded the well-respected Minneapolis-based Institute for Agriculture and Trade Policy twenty-five years ago because he grew up thinking about food.

Well, okay, maybe it isn't as simple as that, but his father was a scientist for the U.S. Department of Agriculture, a role that also moved the family around to various research facilities throughout the country. So when your dad works for the ag department, "you think about food," Ritchie says with a grin.

His thinking about agriculture and food production led him to start college in the late 1960s in biochemistry and biophysics at Iowa State University in Ames.

Though he would graduate with a history and social studies teaching degree instead, "I remained interested in food, ag, all of those subjects," he recalls, because "food is so vital . . . it touches everyone."

He eventually combined this interest with an emerging interest in public policy, not an unusual pursuit during those politically charged times of the late sixties. Meanwhile, like his dad, Ritchie also moved around the country, living at various times in Alaska, Minnesota, and California. His combined interests led to a range of activities, such as creating one of the first food-cooperative networks in Northern California, based extensively on food co-op models he had learned about back in Minnesota.

By the 1980s, Ritchie had returned to the Midwest and was serving as a trade policy analyst for the Minnesota Department of Agriculture, working especially to address, at that time, Ritchie says, "The crisis-level economic and market forces that were threatening family farms and rural communities."

As Ritchie recalls, "We looked at and explored a variety of elements that would make a difference and solve these problems," components such as helping farmers diversify crops and products, and working with farmers to develop broad sustainability overall. He could see that state and federal policies that might help support family farms were sometimes being undercut by worldwide forces, including global trade agreements.

The bottom-line solution, Ritchie discovered: get local and go global—at the same time. As he once told the *Southwest Journal*, connect the local to the global. "If you wanted to protect your food cooperatives, your farmers' markets, your family farmers, your rural communities, you had to work at the local, the state, the federal, and the international level simultaneously."

With that discovery in mind, he created the Institute for Agriculture and Trade Policy, which celebrated its twenty-fifth year in 2011 as a voice for, as its informational materials proclaim, "building sustainable rural communities and healthy food systems."

Though Ritchie would eventually leave the institute to run for elective office in 2006, and now works in the high-demand arena of Minnesota politics, he remains passionate about agriculture and food issues. He couples that passion with humor, too. He knows that public policy, as it relates to agriculture, can be a bit boring at times. Food, on the other hand, seems to always create engaging discussions.

He mentions his friend Martin Teitel, an author and activist. "When Marty's on an airplane and doesn't want to talk to the person next to him, he'll say he works in agriculture. But, if he actually wants to talk to the person, he says he works with food."

131

MAPLE-GLAZED BAKED APPLE

From Beth Dooley,
Minneapolis food writer

Beth Dooley reports that some of the most interesting apple varieties are available only at the farmers' markets, not in stores. These older "heirloom" varieties have been cultivated for flavor and cooking qualities, not because the trees are especially productive or the apples store well. Regent and Keepsake are terrific for baking, and they're just the right size for a dish like this, says Dooley, who serves these baked apples for breakfast as well as dessert.

4 TART APPLES (KEEPSAKE OR
    REGENT WORK WELL)
4 TBSP MAPLE SYRUP
4 TBSP DRIED CRANBERRIES

FRESH APPLE CIDER

Serves 4

1 Preheat the oven to 350°F.

2 Core the apples to within about ½ inch of their bottoms. Peel each apple down to about its middle.

3 Place the apples, bottoms down, in a baking dish, and fill each apple with 1 tablespoon syrup and 1 tablespoon dried cranberries. Pour about ¼ inch of cider into the baking dish. Bake the apples, basting occasionally with the cider, until tender but not mushy, 30–45 minutes.

4 Serve warm with ice cream if desired.

SUMMER FRUIT FOOL

From Jennette Turner,
natural foods educator

Twin Citians love to get out of town and head to any number of pick-your-own berry farms that dot the rural landscape beyond the metro. So here's a recipe to go along with all of those berries folks will bring back. By the way, as Jennette Turner explains, a "fool" is a traditional English dessert made with fruit puree and whipped cream. You can use any kind or combination of summer fruit here; the recipe is very versatile. (Read more about Turner on page 17.) You can also choose fun add-ins (see recipe) as you like, but Turner recommends adding basil to strawberry fool (garnish with basil leaves or pine nuts), adding cinnamon to peach fool; adding amaretto to raspberry fool (garnish with slivered almonds); adding Grand Marnier and cinnamon to plum fool; and adding mint to blackberry fool.

1¼ CUPS HEAVY CREAM
2 CUPS FRESH FRUIT—BERRIES OR
    CHOPPED STONE FRUIT
2–4 TBSP AGAVE SYRUP OR HONEY,
    TO TASTE
1 TSP VANILLA EXTRACT
PINCH OF SALT

OPTIONAL FUN ADD-INS: 1–2 TBSP
LIQUEUR (ORANGE, AMARETTO,
ETC.); 1 TBSP MINCED FRESH
MINT OR BASIL; ½ TSP GROUND
CINNAMON OR FRESHLY GRATED
NUTMEG; OR 2 TSP GRATED
FRESH GINGER OR GINGER JUICE
BERRIES, SLICED FRUIT, OR MINT
LEAVES, FOR GARNISH

Serves 4

1 In a medium bowl, with an electric mixer, whip the cream until it forms soft peaks.

2 Combine the fruit, agave syrup, vanilla, salt, and a fun add-in (if using) in a blender or food processor. Puree until smooth.

3 Fold the fruit puree into the whipped cream and stir gently until smooth. Pour into wineglasses or dessert bowls. Chill before serving.

4 Garnish with a few berries, slices of other fruit, or mint leaves.

Edible Nutrition Tip

For this recipe, Turner also has this nutrition tip: whipping cream made from the milk of grass-fed cows is an excellent source of cancer-fighting conjugated linoleic acid and vitamin D.

NORWEGIAN FRUIT SOUP

From Ann L. Burckhardt,
food writer and cookbook author

"Though I am half-German, half-English, and all American, my faith community includes many families of Norwegian descent," says Ann L. Burckhardt. "For a long time we had a festive smorgasbord every fall, replete with old-country specialties including *fruktsuppe*. As we stirred a batch of this soup one year, the older cook who was guiding me said, 'For Saturday lunch at our house, we like a bowl of warm fruit soup and a slice or two of hot toast.'" As Burckhardt points out, "Like the Italian's beloved minestrone, no two families make this dish quite the same way. So feel free to make your own adaptation."

3 CUPS MIXED DRIED FRUITS, SUCH AS PRUNES, APRICOTS, APPLES, CRANBERRIES, RAISINS, PEARS, AND PEACHES

3 TBSP MINUTE TAPIOCA

½ CUP PEELED SLICED APPLE (OPTIONAL)

1 CUP PITTED FRESH CHERRIES (OPTIONAL)

⅔ CUP GRAPE JUICE OR ⅓ CUP GRAPE JELLY

½ CUP ORANGE JUICE OR APPLE JUICE

2 TBSP FRESH LEMON JUICE

1 TSP GRATED ORANGE ZEST (OPTIONAL)

⅓ CUP GRANULATED SUGAR (OPTIONAL)

CREAM OR VANILLA YOGURT

Serves 6–8

1 Place the dried fruit in a large bowl, cover with 5 cups of water, and let rest, covered, for 1 hour.

2 Transfer the fruit and soaking water to a large saucepan and cook over low heat until the fruit is nearly tender, about 30 minutes.

3 Stir in the tapioca, apple (if using), cherries (if using), grape juice, orange juice, lemon juice, and orange zest (if using). Cook, stirring frequently, until the tapioca is clear and the soup is thickened. Taste and add the sugar if necessary.

4 Serve hot or cold with a dollop of cream or vanilla yogurt on top. Cover any leftover fruit soup and refrigerate to enjoy later warmed in the microwave oven.

Edible Tip

For a touch of spice, add 2 cinnamon sticks to the pan when cooking the fruit in its soaking water. Remove the sticks before serving or storing the soup.

WARTIME CAKE

From Virginia Cherne

Cooking can be a poignant way to recon-nect with family history. This recipe is an example. Virginia Cherne's grandmother, Mary Elizabeth Cherne, made this cake in the small northern Minnesota iron-mining town of Eveleth during World War II, when eggs and butter were rationed. Cherne notes that "the grand-children were served the version without the optional infusion of rum." Virginia Cherne is a cook who lives in Prior Lake, a southern suburb of the Twin Cities.

FOR THE CAKE:
2 CUPS PACKED LIGHT BROWN
   SUGAR
2 CUPS HOT WATER
2 TSP SHORTENING
¾ CUP RAISINS
1 TSP SALT
1 TSP GROUND CINNAMON
1 TSP GROUND CLOVES
3 CUPS ALL-PURPOSE FLOUR

1 TSP BAKING SODA DISSOLVED IN
   2 TSP HOT WATER

FOR A RUM-INFUSED CAKE
(OPTIONAL):
⅓ CUP RUM
1 TBSP LIGHT BROWN SUGAR

Serves 6–8

MAKE THE CAKE:

1 Preheat the oven to 350°F. Lightly grease a Bundt pan or a tube pan.

2 Combine the brown sugar, hot water, and shortening in a 2-quart saucepan. Stir over medium heat until the shortening has melted. Add the raisins, salt, cinnamon, and cloves. Mix and boil for 5 minutes after it first bubbles. Remove from the heat and let cool completely.

3 Stir the flour and baking soda mixture into the raisin mixture and blend well. Pour the batter into the cake pan and bake until a wooden pick inserted in the center comes out clean, about 1 hour. Cool in the pan on a wire rack for 10–15 minutes; then invert onto the rack to cool completely.

IF DESIRED, MAKE A RUM-INFUSED CAKE:

4 While the cake is baking, combine the rum and brown sugar in a small saucepan and heat just until the sugar dissolves completely. After the baked cake has cooled in the pan for about 10 minutes, flip it onto a cooling rack set into a rimmed baking sheet. Using a wooden skewer, poke holes along the top of the cake. Brush the rum and brown sugar mixture over the top of the cake until all the mixture is used up.

THE BEST CHOCOLATE PUDDING EVER

From Elizabeth Ries, co-host of KSTP-TV's Twin Cities Live

This recipe's title is uncharacteristically boastful for a Minnesotan. Explanation? The recipe's author really, *really* likes this pudding. "This dish is for true chocolate lovers, it's so deep, dark, and rich," says Elizabeth Ries, an ardent home cook.

2 CUPS WHOLE MILK
½ CUP PACKED LIGHT BROWN SUGAR
3 TBSP GRANULATED SUGAR
3 TBSP UNSWEETENED COCOA POWDER
3 TBSP CORNSTARCH
¼ TSP SALT

4 OZ FINE-QUALITY SEMISWEET CHOCOLATE, FINELY CHOPPED
1 TSP VANILLA EXTRACT
1 CUP LIGHTLY SWEETENED WHIPPED CREAM

Serves 4

1 Vigorously whisk together ½ cup of the milk and the brown sugar, granulated sugar, cocoa powder, cornstarch, and salt in a medium bowl until blended.

2 Heat the remaining 1½ cups milk in a small saucepan over medium heat. When small bubbles appear on the side of the pan, pour the cocoa mixture into the saucepan and whisk to combine.

3 Cook, whisking, until the pudding thickens, 2–3 minutes. Remove from the heat and whisk in the chopped chocolate and the vanilla.

4 Spoon the pudding into 4 dessert glasses or dishes. Serve warm or chilled and topped with whipped cream.

STEAMED CRANBERRY PUDDING WITH RUM SAUCE

From Jacqueline Gabel, former contributor to Edible Twin Cities

This is a holiday family favorite from Minneapolis native Jacqueline Gabel, a former freelance writer for *Edible Twin Cities* who more recently has been teaching in Korea and traveling through Asia. She says everything she learns while traveling influences how she eats and what she cooks, "but Midwest comfort foods are what I always revert to."

FOR THE PUDDING:
2 CUPS FRESH CRANBERRIES
2 TSP BAKING SODA
½ CUP BOILING WATER
½ CUP MOLASSES
1½ CUPS FLOUR
½ CUP CHOPPED PECANS OR
  WALNUTS

FOR THE SAUCE:
1 CUP SUGAR
½ CUP HEAVY CREAM
1 STICK (8 TBSP) UNSALTED
  BUTTER, AT ROOM
  TEMPERATURE
2 TBSP RUM OR VANILLA EXTRACT
  (OR A BIT OF BOTH)

Serves 8–10

MAKE THE PUDDING:

1 Place the cranberries and baking soda in a large heatproof bowl, pour the boiling water over them, and stir to combine. Fold in the molasses, flour, and nuts, and mix well. Pour the batter into a 1½-quart round glass casserole dish.

2 Wrap a piece of wax paper around the dish and tie it with string around the top. Place a wire rack in a deep pot (a stockpot or soup pot works well). Pour water into the pot up to, but not over, the rack (the water should not touch the casserole dish), and place the casserole dish on top of the rack.

3 Place the stockpot over medium-high heat. Once the water begins to boil, partially cover the pot and steam for 1½ hours. (Keep hot to boiling water ready to add to the pot if the water on the bottom gets too low.) When finished, the pudding will be about 4 inches high, tapering on the sides.

MEANWHILE, MAKE THE SAUCE:

4 Combine the sugar, cream, butter, and rum in a double boiler. Set over medium heat and cook slowly, until the sugar has melted. Keep warm.

SCOTCH PIE

From Dan Oskey, bartender, The Strip Club Meat & Fish Restaurant

Make no mistake—the temperatures are cold in Minnesota in December and January. So, in a past winter issue of *Edible Twin Cities*, the magazine turned to bartender Dan Oskey for recommendations on beverages that would warm up a Minnesota winter. He delivered several invigorating options, including the recipe listed here. Oskey, whose honors include being named Twin Cities' best bartender by *City Pages*, named this drink in honor of its main ingredient: Dewar's Scotch. Cheers.

2 OZ DEWAR'S SCOTCH WHISKEY
½ OZ DOMAIN DE CANTON GINGER LIQUEUR
½ OZ APFELKORN (GERMAN APPLE SCHNAPPS)
½ OZ CHERRY HEERING (CHERRY LIQUEUR)

1 TSP ROSEMARY/MAPLE SYRUP (RECIPE FOLLOWS)
BRANDIED CHERRY, FOR GARNISH

Makes 1 drink

1   In a pint glass filled with ice, combine the whiskey, ginger liqueur, apple schnapps, cherry liqueur, and rosemary/maple syrup. Shake the contents and strain into a martini glass. Garnish with a brandied cherry.

ROSEMARY/MAPLE SYRUP

1 CUP REAL MAPLE SYRUP
1 TBSP FINELY CHOPPED FRESH ROSEMARY

Makes about 1 cup

1   Bring the maple syrup and rosemary to a simmer in a small saucepan. Let cool and strain out the rosemary. Pour into a sterilized mason jar. Store in the refrigerator for up to 2 weeks.

MIDNIGHT GARDEN MOCHA

From Montana, River Rock
Coffee, St. Peter

This is a delectable little drink to make you warm and cozy when the temperature drops. This recipe was submitted by Montana, who works for River Rock Coffee in St. Peter, which is about an hour south of the Twin Cities. "We get the lavender from one of our farmer partners and we make the simple syrup in our kitchen at River Rock," says Montana. "The perfect combination of chocolate and lavender." River Rock Coffee is committed to, as its website proclaims, "fresh, organic, and sustainable. We want people to eat good food."

2 TBSP GHIRARDELLI GROUND
    CHOCOLATE
2 SHOTS BREWED ESPRESSO
1½ TBSP HOMEMADE LAVENDER
    SIMPLE SYRUP (RECIPE FOLLOWS)

ABOUT 1 CUP WHOLE MILK,
    STEAMED
WHIPPED CREAM

Makes 1 drink

1 Put the ground chocolate in your favorite mug. Pull two perfect shots of espresso and pour them into your mug as well. Stir until the chocolate powder is dissolved.

2 Add the homemade lavender simple syrup; then pour in the steamed milk. Give it a final stir and top with whipped cream.

HOMEMADE LAVENDER SIMPLE SYRUP

1 CUP ORGANIC WHITE SUGAR

3 TBSP LOCAL ORGANIC DRIED
    LAVENDER

Makes about 1 cup

1 Bring the sugar and 1 cup of water to a boil in a small saucepan. Once it has reached a boil, reduce the heat and simmer for 10 minutes. Remove from the heat and stir in the lavender. Cover and let cool to room temperature. Strain out the lavender and pour the syrup into a sterilized jar. Store in the refrigerator for up to 3 weeks.

THE BRIMLEY

From Dan Oskey, bartender,
The Strip Club Meat & Fish
Restaurant

Edible Twin Cities asked bartender Dan Oskey for recommendations on beverages that would spice up holiday gatherings and be a cure for the common Minnesota winter. He delivered several awesome options, including the recipe listed here. Oskey named this drink "The Brimley" because it has an oatmeal-and-cinnamon-like taste that reminds him of famous actor and Quaker Oats pitchman Wilford Brimley.

2 OZ OLD OVERHOLT RYE WHISKEY
½ OZ LUXARDO AMARO ABANO
 (ITALIAN BITTER LIQUEUR)
½ OZ VELVET FALERNUM (CLOVE
 AND ALMOND LIQUEUR WITH A
 TOUCH OF CITRUS)

PINCH OF GROUND CINNAMON
CINNAMON STICK, FOR GARNISH

Makes 1 drink

1 In a pint glass half-filled with ice, combine the rye, amaro, Velvet Falernum, and cinnamon. Shake the contents and pour into a lowball glass. Garnish with a cinnamon stick.

THE RECIPE

From Laura French, contributor
to Edible Twin Cities

Minnesota and especially Wisconsin are sometimes cited as states with some of the highest alcohol consumption in the nation, which is not necessarily a statistic we're proud of. On the other hand, Minnesota also has been dubbed "The Land of 10,000 Treatment Centers." That's a good thing, right? Either way, here's a drink that's especially yummy at holiday time, from Laura French, a Minneapolis freelance writer. She says a former co-worker gave her this recipe and called it "homemade Bailey's." French dubbed it "The Recipe," after the concoction made by the elderly sisters on *The Waltons*.

2 CUPS HEAVY CREAM
3 TBSP CHOCOLATE SYRUP
1½ TSP VANILLA EXTRACT
2 LARGE EGGS

1 (14 OZ) CAN SWEETENED
 CONDENSED MILK
1½ CUPS CHEAP WHISKEY

Serves 12

1 Combine the cream, chocolate syrup, vanilla, eggs, and 5 tablespoons of water in a blender. With the machine running, add the condensed milk, then the whiskey. Blend longer for a thicker mixture. Chill and serve. *Note:* The eggs in this recipe are not cooked. If salmonella is a concern in your area, do not make this drink.

CRANBERRY MARGARITAS

From Jacqueline Gabel, former contributor to Edible Twin Cities

This is the perfect holiday cocktail: merry red, refreshing, and packed with spirited cheer. Making the cranberry puree fills the house with the cheery scent of bubbling berries and orange. It takes but a minute to toss together. This recipe is from a past issue of *Edible Twin Cities*.

Edible Fact

Twin Citians are lucky enough to live close to southern Wisconsin's cranberry country, so cranberry options—fresh or frozen—abound for area residents. Recipe author Gabel's favorite brand is Sno Pac organic frozen cranberries. Sno Pac is a family-owned Minnesota company that has been growing and freezing organic products for more than one hundred years.

FOR THE CRANBERRY PUREE:
1 CUP PACKED LIGHT BROWN SUGAR
1 CUP ORANGE JUICE
12 OZ FRESH OR FROZEN CRANBERRIES

FOR THE MARGARITAS:
¼ CUP GRANULATED SUGAR
½ TSP GRATED ORANGE ZEST
9 OZ TEQUILA
9 OZ FRESH LIME JUICE
3 OZ COINTREAU
3 CUPS CRUSHED ICE

Serves 6

MAKE THE CRANBERRY PUREE:

1 Combine the brown sugar and orange juice in a medium saucepan. Bring to a boil over high heat, stir in the cranberries, and boil for about 1 minute. Reduce the heat to a simmer and cook until the cranberries burst, about 15 minutes. Remove from the heat and cool to room temperature. Puree until smooth in a blender and refrigerate (right in the blender) until well chilled.

MAKE THE MARGARITAS:

2 Toss together the sugar and orange zest in a small bowl and pour onto a plate. Wet the rims of 6 cocktail glasses and dip into the orange sugar to coat. Set aside.

3 To the blender with the cooled cranberry puree, add the tequila, lime juice, and Cointreau. Blend; then add enough crushed ice to make a smooth but icy drink. Pour into the sugar-rimmed glasses and serve immediately.

AZTEC CHILE HOT CHOCOLATE

From Jacqueline Gabel, former contributor to Edible Twin Cities

Chile lights a little fire under this warming sweet drink. Inspired by the early Aztec rendition (sans sugar), this recipe blends smooth, rich chocolate with fragrant cinnamon, sparked with a touch of Aztec heat. Not a bad way to warm up on a cold Minnesota day. Indeed, this recipe appeared in a past winter issue of *Edible Twin Cities.*

½ VANILLA BEAN
3 CUPS WHOLE MILK
PINCH OF CAYENNE PEPPER
1 CINNAMON STICK

2½ OZ BITTERSWEET CHOCOLATE, FINELY CHOPPED OR GRATED

Serves 2

1 Split the vanilla bean in half along its inner seam lengthwise. Place the vanilla bean, milk, cayenne, and cinnamon stick in a medium saucepan. Heat over medium heat. Watch for little bubbles to appear around the edges of the pan so the milk just scalds but does not boil.

2 Whisk in the chocolate a little at a time, stirring until it has melted into the milk. Remove from the heat and let steep for about 10 minutes. Remove and discard the vanilla bean. Pour into mugs and serve hot.

ICED LEMON TEA

From Ann L. Burckhardt, food writer and cookbook author

Many Minnesota cooks keep a pitcher of iced tea in the refrigerator from the first hot day of June right through muggy August. This iced-tea version tastes distinctly like summer. "You never know when a family member will come home, looking for something cold and refreshing," says Ann L. Burckhardt. "Or someone will stop by, then stay for a chat and a glass of iced tea. I prefer Yorkshire Gold tea for this summer special."

4 BAGS BLACK TEA
4 CUPS BOILING WATER
⅔ CUP FROZEN LEMONADE
   CONCENTRATE (½ OF A 12-OZ
   CARTON)
3 TBSP SUGAR

3 CUPS COLD TAP WATER
LEMONS SLICES OR MINT SPRIGS,
   FOR GARNISH

Serves 8

1 Place the tea bags in a 2-quart refrigerator pitcher. Pour in the boiling water and let steep for 10 minutes. Add the lemonade concentrate and stir until it melts. Stir in the sugar and cold water. Store, covered, in the refrigerator. Serve over ice in tall glasses. Garnish the glasses with a half slice of lemon or a sprig of mint.

DRINK-SICLE

From Carol J. Butler,
Wisconsin food writer

During Minnesota and Wisconsin winters, neither fruit nor leaves grow on our trees, Carol Butler, a food writer in Superior, Wisconsin, reminds us. So in her family, she relies on "the family snowbirds—Grandpa and Grandma, who flee the cold every winter and return briefly for the holidays, arms laden with boxes of citrus picked from their fair-weather trees." This fruit has seeds, Butler says, so the best thing to do with these oranges is to juice them, "which I do, happily." And, she says, she sometimes will make this recipe. So get out your martini shaker and get ready to shake it like you mean it. This frothy, dreamy drink is like a party favor in a glass for kids and grown-ups alike—and even pretty good for you, too.

6–8 ICE CUBES
2 CUPS ORANGE JUICE (4–6 ORANGES)
⅓ CUP WHOLE MILK
½ TSP VANILLA EXTRACT

1 TBSP RAW SUGAR
ORANGE SLICES, FOR GARNISH (OPTIONAL)

Serves 2

1 Combine the ice, orange juice, milk, vanilla, and sugar in a martini shaker, and shake it like you mean it! Pour into 2 glasses and serve with straws. Garnish with orange slices if desired.

FARMERS' MARKETS

MINNEAPOLIS FARMERS MARKET

This giant market on North Lyndale Avenue on the edge of downtown Minneapolis features local fruits, vegetables, farmstead items, and other products from the Central Minnesota Vegetable Growers Association, a member-based, nonprofit organization with more than two hundred members. The Lyndale Market is open seven days a week, from mid-April until mid-November, with many vendors continuing to sell on Saturdays throughout the winter months. An additional market, the Nicollet Mall Market, is open on Thursdays from May through October.

312 East Lyndale Avenue North, Minneapolis, MN 55405
(612) 333-1718
MplsFarmersMarket.com

ST. PAUL FARMERS' MARKET

Established in 1853, the St. Paul Farmers' Market is open every Saturday in Lowertown. Beyond the Saturday Lowertown market, the 145-member St. Paul Growers' Association has twenty-two markets throughout the Twin Cities metro area, some on weekdays, some on weekends, most of them seasonal.

290 Fifth Street East, St. Paul, MN 55101
(651) 227-6856
StPaulFarmersMarket.com

NEIGHBORHOOD FARMERS' MARKETS

Neighborhood farmers' markets in the Twin Cities and suburbs abound. Minnesota Grown, a program of the Minnesota Department of Agriculture, lists more than 150 farmers' markets statewide. The list is too long to mention here, but these are three of our favorites:

KINGFIELD FARMERS MARKET

Small space, big crowds: this bustling market, open Sundays from late May through October, nourishes

Minneapolis's Kingfield neighborhood with local produce, garden plants, free-range meats, cheese, honey, coffee, and more.

4310 Nicollet Avenue South, Minneapolis, MN 55409
(612) 823-4550, (612) 207-7893
KingfieldFarmersMarket.org

MIDTOWN FARMERS MARKET

This vibrant market is one of the most accessible, too: it is on both the bus and light-rail lines and also has plenty of free parking, even though it's in the heart of the city, just off East Lake Street. Vendors sell only items grown or made in Minnesota or Wisconsin. The market is open Saturdays, early May through October, and Tuesdays, early June through October.

East Lake Street and Twenty-Second Avenue South,
by Highway 55/Hiawatha, Minneapolis, MN 55407
(612) 724-7457
MidtownFarmersMarket.org

MILL CITY FARMERS MARKET

Open Saturdays from early May through mid-October, this market, as Minnesota Grown reports, was the first to focus on locally grown, seasonal foods from sustainable and organic farmers and small businesses in the region.

704 South Second Street, Minneapolis, MN 55401
(612) 341-7580
MillCityFarmersMarket.org

FOOD CO-OPS

The Twin Cities are blessed with thirteen community- and member-owned food co-ops, in fifteen locations throughout the metro area. "Food co-ops and cooperatives in general thrive in this state," says Mark Ritchie, Minnesota's secretary of state and founder of the Minneapolis-based Institute for Agriculture and Trade Policy.

In a recent *Edible Twin Cities* article on forty years of food co-ops in the Twin Cities, Ritchie, talking about all types of co-ops, pointed out, "Minnesota ranks number

one in sheer numbers of cooperatives and our residents enjoy the tremendous benefits co-ops bring." Ritchie says that Minnesota's cooperatives (all co-ops, not just food co-ops) generate more than $34 million in revenue and provide jobs for forty-six thousand Minnesota residents. Minnesota hosted the nation's first credit unions (i.e., Agribank, FCB), farm co-ops (Land O'Lakes), and health care cooperatives (Health Partners).

CITY CENTER MARKET

City Center Market in Cambridge, just north of the Twin Cities, is a natural foods cooperative grocery store that has served Cambridge and surrounding communities for thirty-plus years.

122 North Buchanan Street. Cambridge, MN 55008
(763) 689-4640
CityCenterMarket.coop

EASTSIDE FOOD CO-OP—MINNEAPOLIS

Eastside opened in 2003 in Northeast Minneapolis and now has more than twenty-six hundred member-owners.

2551 Central Avenue, Minneapolis, MN 55418
(612) 788-0950
EastsideFood.coop

HAMPDEN PARK CO-OP—ST. PAUL

This co-op was legally formed in 1990, though its roots date back to the 1970s with the former St. Anthony Park Foods and Green Grass Grocery.

928 Raymond Avenue, St. Paul, MN 55114
(651) 646-6686
Hampdenparkcoop.com

HARVEST MOON NATURAL FOODS CO-OP

Located in Long Lake/Orono in the Twin Cities' western suburbs, Harvest Moon opened in 2010.

Northeast corner of West Wayzata Boulevard and
Willow Drive, Long Lake, MN 55356
(952) 345-3300
HarvestMoon.coop

JUST FOOD CO-OP

In Northfield, just south of the Twin Cities, Just Food Co-op was founded, as its website explains, "due in large part, to our community's desire to have greater access to locally grown food and support local, sustainable farmers."

516 South Water Street, Northfield, MN 55057
(507) 650-0106
JustFood.coop

LAKEWINDS NATURAL FOODS

The western suburbs of the Twin Cities are well served by Lakewinds Natural Foods, a full-service cooperative grocery serving the west metro suburban Twin Cities for more thirty years.

17501 Minnetonka Boulevard, Minnetonka, MN 55345
(952) 473-0292

435 Pond Promenade, Chanhassen, MN 55317
(952) 697-3366
Lakewinds.com

LINDEN HILLS CO-OP

Established in 1976, this co-op moved into a sleek new facility in 2010.

3815 Sunnyside Avenue, Minneapolis, MN 55410
(612) 922-1159
LindenHills.coop

MISSISSIPPI MARKET NATURAL FOOD CO-OP

Mississippi Market has been consumer owned and controlled since 1979, and now has two inviting St. Paul locations.

622 Selby Avenue, St. Paul, MN 55104
(651) 310-9499

1500 West Seventh Street, St. Paul, MN 55102
(651) 690-0507
MSMarket.coop

RIVER MARKET COMMUNITY CO-OP

In the scenic river town of Stillwater, just east of St. Paul, River Market is a full-line food market that offers the largest selection of organic and natural foods in the St. Croix Valley.

221 North Main Street, Suite 1, Stillwater, MN 55082
(651) 439-0366
RiverMarket.coop

SEWARD CO-OP GROCERY & DELI

Seward was one of the first co-ops in the area, opening in 1972 on the corner of Twenty-Second and Franklin Avenues, with the help of members from what was then called North Country Co-op. In 2009, Seward opened the doors of its new home, a gorgeous, 25,600-square-foot building, also on Franklin Avenue. The co-op also now has more than eighty-eight hundred members.

2823 East Franklin Avenue, Minneapolis, MN 55406
(612) 338-2465
Seward.coop

ST. PETER FOOD CO-OP & DELI

Located in the Minnesota River Valley south of the Twin Cities, this co-op was established more than thirty years ago and recently opened a beautiful new location.

228 Mulberry Street, St. Peter, MN 56082
(507) 934-4880
StPeterFood.coop

VALLEY NATURAL FOODS

Valley Natural Foods, in the southern suburb of Burnsville, is, as its website states, "a community-owned cooperative, providing healthy choices since 1977."

13750 County Road 11, Burnsville, MN 55337
(952) 891-1212
ValleyNaturalFoods.coop

THE WEDGE CO-OP

Another pioneer in the early food co-op movement, The Wedge Co-op has served its members and neighborhoods since 1974. In a relatively small space in South Minneapolis, this co-op attracts big numbers. For example, the Wedge now has more than fourteen thousand members. Plus, in 2010, the *Star Tribune* reported that the co-op's total annual "patronage refund" to its members hit $1 million for the first time, marking one of the largest such distributions in the country. The *Star Tribune* also reported that, based on sales, the Wedge is one of the nation's largest single-store natural foods cooperatives.

2105 Lyndale Avenue South, Minneapolis, MN 55405
(612) 871-3993
Wedge.coop

FARMERS, GROWERS, MARKETS, SPECIALTY SHOPS, AND OTHERS

CLANCEY'S MEATS & FISH

This butcher shop in the heart of Minneapolis' Linden Hills neighborhood offers locally sourced products from Minnesota family farms. Read more about Clancey's and its owner, Kristin Tombers, on page 87.

4307 Upton Avenue South, Minneapolis, MN 55410
(612) 926-0222
ClanceysMeats.com

EICHTEN'S HIDDEN ACRES

An excellent source for buffalo/bison meat, Eichten's has one of the largest American bison herds in the state. Plus find cheese, sausages, wild rice, honey, and more. Eichten's also sells at area farmers' markets.

Located between Center City and Schafer, MN, on Highway 8
(651) 257-4752; (651) 257-1566
SpecialtyCheese.com

FEATHERSTONE FRUITS & VEGETABLES

Featherstone provides certified organic fruits and vegetables that are available through CSA shares and at stores from Minneapolis to Chicago.

43090 City Park Road, Rushford, MN 55971
(507) 864-2400
FeatherstoneFarm.com

FERNDALE MARKET

Operated by a family of farmers, Ferndale specializes in free-range turkey but also offers a full line of local meats, specialty items, and seasonal produce. Ferndale also has partnerships with area producers to provide an impressive range of local, sustainable foods.

31659 County Road 24 Boulevard (just west of Highway 52 at County Road 24), Cannon Falls, MN 55009
(507) 263-4556
FerndaleMarketOnline.com

GARDENS OF EAGAN

This hundred-acre, urban-edge farm, which is owned by the Wedge Co-op, provides certified organic produce and garden transplants to the Twin Cities and region. It also is an educational resource to consumers and farmers through its nonprofit Organic Field School. Its produce is available through a local organic distributor and many retail co-ops, and at Midtown and Fulton Farmers Markets in Minneapolis.

25494 Highview Avenue, Farmington, MN 55024
(952) 985-7233
GardensofEagan.com

GOLDEN FIG FINE FOODS
This specialty shop on Grand Avenue in St. Paul is loaded with locally produced, gourmet products.

790 Grand Avenue, St. Paul, MN 55105
(651) 602-0144
GoldenFig.com

GRASS FED CATTLE CO.
This cooperative of area farmers sells beef that is local, free-range, antibiotic-free, and 100 percent grass fed.

3939 West Fiftieth Street, Edina, MN 55424
(612) 581-7787
GrassFedCattleCo.com

GRASSROOTS GOURMET
Grassroots specializes in regional artisan cheeses, meat, dairy, and general groceries.

920 East Lake Street, Stall 130, Midtown Global Market, Minneapolis, MN 55407
(612) 871-6947
E-mail: potts992@msn.com

HOPE CREAMERY
Located in southern Minnesota in the tiny town of Hope, this creamery remains one of the only independently owned creameries in the state. Hope's Grade A butter is available at a number of restaurants and food co-ops in the Twin Cities.

PO Box 42, 9043 Southwest Thirty-Seventh Avenue, Hope, MN 56046
(507) 451-2029

LOCAL D'LISH
The owners of this neighborhood local foods grocery store on the edge of downtown, Ann and Yulin Yin, think of their store as a farmers' market in a retail format. As they state on the store's website: "We strive to offer you the best products that Minnesota and the 'heartland' [have] to offer."

208 North First Street, Minneapolis, MN 55401
(612) 886-3047
LocalDLish.com

MASTEL'S
Your favorite healthy ingredients and related products abound here: farm-fresh eggs, gluten-free ingredients, vegetable juicers, vitamins and supplements, herbs, homeopathic remedies, and more.

1526 St. Clair Avenue, St. Paul, MN 55105
(651) 690-1692
Mastels.com

MIDTOWN GLOBAL MARKET
We love this international marketplace in the heart of Minneapolis's urban-core neighborhoods of Phillips and Powderhorn. Stroll this charming indoor market and discover specialty groceries; fresh produce; ethnic restaurants; baked goods; arts, gifts, and jewelry boutiques; and more.

920 East Lake Street, Minneapolis, MN 55407
(612) 872-4041
MidtownGlobalMarket.org

PASTURELAND DAIRY COOPERATIVE
PastureLand's 100 percent grass-fed organic dairy products, from its farms in southeastern Minnesota, are handcrafted by artisan butter and cheese makers. Order online or check PastureLand's website for its retail locations.

PastureLand Cooperative, W3443 Country Highway West, Belleville, WI 53508
(608) 438-1632
PastureLand.coop

PASTURES A PLENTY FARM & CO.
This farm in west-central Minnesota is an excellent source for farm-fresh foods. It is home to free-range chickens, grass-fed cows, and pasture-raised pigs. Its products are available at several Twin Cities food co-ops and restaurants.

4075 and 4077 110th Avenue Northeast, Kerkhoven, MN 56252
(320) 367-2061, (866) 290-2469
PasturesAPlenty.com

RIVERBEND FARM

A certified organic vegetable farm about thirty miles west of Minneapolis, Riverbend provides wholesale produce to outlets throughout the Twin Cities such as restaurants and food co-ops, and directly to consumers through its CSA. Read more about Greg and Mary Reynolds and their Riverbend Farm on page 80.
5405 Calder Avenue Southeast, Delano, MN
(763) 972-3295
RbFCSA.com

STAR PRAIRIE TROUT FARM

Less than an hour from the Twin Cities, Star Prairie Trout supplies its fresh fish to a number of food co-ops, supermarkets, farmers' markets, wholesalers, and restaurants in the region.
400 Hill Avenue, Star Prairie, WI 54026
(715) 248-3633
StarPrairieTrout.com

THOUSAND HILLS CATTLE COMPANY

Thousand Hills works with more than seventy family farms that raise 100 percent grass-fed beef. Thousand Hills supplies its beef to local food stores and restaurants and directly to consumers. Home delivery is available throughout Minnesota.
P.O. Box 68, Cannon Falls, MN 55009
(507) 263-4001
ThousandHillsCattleCo.com

TRADEWINDS SPICE COMPANY

This Stillwater store offers spices and seasonings from around the world but also seeks out regional specialties and products from small producers.
Historic Brick Alley Building
423 South Main Street, Stillwater, MN 55082
(651) 351-0422; (877) BE-SPICY; (877) 237-7429
TradewindsSpice.com

UNTIEDT'S VEGETABLE FARM

A major presence at the Minneapolis Farmers Market, Untiedt's, a family farm operation in Montrose and Waverly, also sells produce at several roadside stands in the Twin Cities' western suburbs.
4750 Twenty-Fifth Street SW, Waverly, MN 55390
(763) 658-4672
UntiedtsWeGrowforYou.com

WHOLE GRAIN MILLING CO.

Whole Grain Milling grows and processes certified organic grains and provides food co-ops in the Twin Cities, Greater Minnesota, Wisconsin, and South Dakota with fresh, high-quality whole-grain products direct from its certified organic farm.
1579 120th Avenue, Welcome, MN 56181
(507) 728-8489
WholeGrainMilling.net

WHOLEFARMCOOP.COM

Order your groceries online with this Long Prairie, Minnesota-based service, and have them delivered to one of several Twin Cities–area churches that serve as drop sites.
33 Second Street South, Suite #102, Long Prairie, MN 56347
(320) 732-3023
WholeFarmCoop.com

WILD RUN SALMON

Matt Oxford, who splits his time between South St. Paul and Fritz Creek, Alaska, sells his Alaskan salmon at several area farmers' markets: Nicollet Mall, White Bear Lake, Mill City, Fulton, and Kingfield. His motto: "From our boat to your table."
(651) 999-9410
WildRunSalmon.com

BEVERAGES
COCKTAILS

If you're on the hunt for hard-to-find ingredients for your favorite cocktails, our friend Dan Oskey, bartender at the Strip Club Meat & Fish restaurant in St. Paul, has recommendations. We tend to listen to Oskey, who was named bartender of the year in 2010 by City Pages. By the way, he also has a drink recipe or two in this book (see pages 141 and 144). He says you can find all the alcohol ingredients you're looking for at any of these three places:

SURDYK'S
You can't miss this northeast Minneapolis landmark—it's huge. The selection matches the store's size.

303 East Hennepin Avenue, Minneapolis, MN 55414
(612) 379-3232
Surdyks.com

THOMAS LIQUORS
Located on the western end of historic Grand Avenue, in the lovely Macalester-Groveland neighborhood of St. Paul, this store focuses on fine wines and craft beers.

1941 Grand Avenue, St. Paul, MN 55105
(651) 699-1860
ThomasLiquor.com

THE WINE MARKET
In the St. Paul suburb of Mendota Heights, this store specializes in wines—and lots of them.

720 Main Street, #101, Mendota Heights, MN 55118
(651) 452-9463
TheWineMarket.us

BEER
Big, small, and microbreweries seem to be everywhere these days, and lots of area liquor stores have fabulous selections of local beers. Plus, a whole lot of folks here like to brew their own. Here's a list of some favorites:

BREWERIES
BRAU BROTHERS BREWING CO.
201 South First Street, Lucan, MN 56255
(507) 747-BEER
BrauBeer.com

FLAT EARTH BREWING CO.
2035 Benson Avenue, St. Paul, MN 55116
(651) 698-1945
FlatEarthBrewing.com

FULTON BREWING CO.
414 Sixth Avenue North, Minneapolis, MN 55401
(612) 333-3208
FultonBeer.com

HARRIET BREWING
3036 Minnehaha Avenue, Minneapolis, MN 55406
(612) 225-2184
HarrietBrewing.com

LAKE SUPERIOR BREWING CO.
2711 West Superior Street, Duluth, MN 55806
(218) 723-4000
LakeSuperiorBrewing.com

LIFT BRIDGE BREWERY
1900 Tower Drive, Stillwater, MN 55082
(888) 430-BEER (2337)
LiftBridgeBrewery.com

MANTORVILLE BREWING CO.
101 East Fifth Street, Mantorville, MN 55955
(651) 387-0708
MantorvilleBeer.com

AUGUST SCHELL BREWING CO.
1860 Schell Road, New Ulm, MN 56073
(507) 354-5528, (800) 770-5020
SchellsBrewery.com

SUMMIT BREWING COMPANY
910 Montreal Circle, St. Paul, MN 55102
(651) 265-7800
SummitBrewing.com

SURLY BREWING CO.
4811 Dusharme Drive, Brooklyn Center, MN 55429
(763) 535-3330
SurlyBrewing.com

LIQUOR STORES SPECIALIZING IN BEER
ALE JAIL (AND WINE THIEF)

1787 St. Clair Avenue, St. Paul, MN 55105
(651) 698-9463
WineThief.net

THE FOUR FIRKINS

5630 Thirty-Sixth Street, St. Louis Park, MN 55416
TheFourFirkins.com

FOR THE HOME BREWER
MIDWEST SUPPLIES

You'll find extensive home-brewing and wine-making supplies here.

5825 Excelsior Boulevard, Minneapolis, MN 55416
(952) 925-9854
MidwestSupplies.com

THE NORTHERN BREWER

Whether you're a beginner or an experienced brewer, you'll find an array of home-brewing kits, supplies, and equipment. Two locations:

1150 Grand Avenue, St. Paul, MN 55105

6021 Lyndale Avenue South, Minneapolis, MN 55419
(651) 223-6114
NorthernBrewer.com

BEER WEBSITES
MINNESOTA BEER

MNBeer.com

MINNESOTA CRAFT BREWER'S GUILD

MNCraftBrew.org

WINE
VINEYARDS, WINERIES
ALEXIS BAILLY VINEYARD

18200 Kirby Avenue, Hastings, MN 55033
(651) 437-1413
ABVWines.com

CANNON RIVER WINERY

421 Mill Street West, Cannon Falls, MN 55009
(507) 263-7400, (507) 755-9156
CannonRiverWinery.com

CROFUT FAMILY VINEYARD

21646 Langford Avenue South (on Highway 13) Jordan, MN 55352
(952) 492-3227
CrofutWinery.com

FORESTEDGE WINERY

35295 State 64, LaPorte, MN 56461
(218) 224-3535, (218) 224-2668
ForestedgeWinery.com

MORGAN CREEK VINEYARDS

23707 478th Avenue, New Ulm, MN 56073
(507) 947-3547
MorganCreekVineyards.com

NORTHERN VINEYARDS

223 Main Street North, Stillwater, MN 55082
(651) 430-1032
NorthernVineyards.com

SAINT CROIX VINEYARDS

6428 Manning Avenue, Stillwater, MN 55082
(651) 430-3310
SCVWines.com

SEVEN HAWKS VINEYARDS

17 North Street, Fountain City, WI 54629
(866) 946-3741
SevenHawksVineyards.com

WINE WEBSITE
MINNESOTA GRAPE GROWERS ASSOCIATION

MNGrapeGrowers.com

COFFEE

COFFEE & TEA LTD.

*2730 West Forty-Third Street, Linden Hills,
Minneapolis, MN 55410*

*2000 NE Court, First Floor in Sears, Mall of America,
Bloomington, MN 55425
(612) 920-6344; (952) 854-2883
CoffeeandTeaLtd.com*

PEACE COFFEE

*3262 Minnehaha Avenue South, Minneapolis, MN 55406
(612) 877-7760
PeaceCoffeeShop.com*

PEOPLES ORGANIC COFFEE & WINE CAFÉ

*Galleria-Edina
3545 Galleria, Edina, MN 55435
(952) 426-1856
PeoplesOrganic.com*

ORGANIZATIONS

INSTITUTE FOR AGRICULTURE AND TRADE POLICY (IATP)

This Minneapolis-based organization recently commemorated 25 years of being a public policy voice in Minnesota and Washington, D.C. for building sustainable rural communities and healthy food systems.

*2105 First Avenue South, Minneapolis, MN 55404
(612) 870-0453*

*1100 Fifteenth Street NW, 11th Floor, Washington, DC 20005
(202) 222-0749
IATP.org*

LAND STEWARDSHIP PROJECT

This active, grassroots group of three thousand members—farmers and rural and urban residents—works to foster an ethic of stewardship for farmland, promote sustainable agriculture, and develop sustainable communities. Though based in Minnesota, the group also works in Wisconsin, Iowa, and North and South Dakota.

*Twin Cities Policy Office
821 East Thirty-Fifth Street, Suite 200, Minneapolis, MN 55407
(612) 722-6377
LandStewardshipProject.org*

MINNESOTA FARMERS UNION

For seventy years, this membership-based group has worked to protect and enhance the economic interests and quality of life of family farmers and rural communities.

*600 County Road D West, Suite 14, St. Paul, MN 55112
(651) 639-1223, (800) 969-3380
MFU.org*

MINNESOTA FOOD ASSOCIATION

Minnesota Food Association is dedicated to growing farmers and growing food. The Big River Farms Program of MFA operates an immigrant and minority farmer-training program together with a CSA and wholesale distribution service. MFA provides farmers with the skills and knowledge to operate their own viable organic and sustainable vegetable farms, while providing fresh, organic produce to local consumers by the farmers-in-training.

*14220-B Ostlund Trail North, Marine on St. Croix, MN 55047
(651) 433-3676
MNFoodAssociation.org*

MINNESOTA GROWN

The Minnesota Grown Program is all about promoting local foods. A part of the Minnesota Department of Agriculture, Minnesota Grown publishes an extensive annual directory that includes farmers' markets, CSA farms, garden centers, orchards, berry farms, Christmas tree farms, and more.

*Minnesota Department of Agriculture
Minnesota Grown Program
625 Robert Street North, St. Paul, MN 55155
(651) 201-6539
MinnesotaGrown.com*

MINNESOTA INSTITUTE FOR SUSTAINABLE AGRICULTURE (MISA)

MISA is a University of Minnesota–based partnership of agricultural organizations and interests.

*University of Minnesota
411 Borlaug Hall, 1991 Upper Buford Circle,
St. Paul, MN 55108
(612) 625-8235
www.MISA.UMN.edu*

SUSTAINABLE FARMING ASSOCIATION OF MINNESOTA
SFA of Minnesota supports the development and
enhancement of sustainable farming systems through
farmer-to-farmer networking, innovation, demonstration,
and education.

Box 192, Princeton, MN 55371
(763) 260-0209
SFA-MN.org

WOMEN'S ENVIRONMENTAL INSTITUTE (WEI)
WEI is an environmental research, renewal, and retreat
center designed to, as its website explains, "create
and share knowledge about environmental issues and
policies relevant to women, children, and identified
communities especially affected by environmental
injustices." Through its retreat and conference center,
farm program, and various educational programs, WEI
promotes and supports agricultural justice, organic

and sustainable agriculture, ecological awareness, and
activism that influences public policy and promotes
social change.

P.O. Box 128, North Branch, MN 55056
(651) 583-0705
W-E-I.org

WOMEN WHO REALLY COOK
This networking organization for women in the food
business in the Twin Cities area meets monthly in
various locations. The group's name is a takeoff on the
name of a local all-female musical group, Women Who
Cook.

(612) 670-6683
rgilsrud5@aol.com
WWRC.info

ACKNOWLEDGMENTS FROM TRACEY RYDER

Edible Communities would like to thank Carole Topalian for her visually enticing photographs—whether showing off the talented people and distinct neighborhoods that define the Twin Cities area or highlighting the recipes themselves. They all come together to paint a compelling story about the food from this rich and diverse midwestern region.

We would also like to thank the team at *Edible Twin Cities* for their hard work and dedication to this book, especially Mark Weber, publisher, and Angelo Gentile, editor. Both gentlemen, along with their staff, embraced this project with grace, enthusiasm, and tremendous insight into the communities where they live and work, and the product they created is all the better for their efforts.

A special thanks goes to the Edible Communities team, who spent long hours pulling every detail together to make this project a solid success. Without their efforts, this book would literally not exist. They are: our spectacularly brilliant managing editor, Elissa Altman; Jill Lightner, the most amazing example of a grace-under-pressure recipe developer; Varanya Vadakan, Kelly Day, and Kellyn Baez, who kept the ship sailing while the rest of us spent weeks in the kitchen; and the ever-talented Marjorie Garland, who was somehow able to prep, cook, and clean up after a dozen or more recipes each day without losing her focus or her enthusiasm.

Last but certainly not least, we would like to send big hugs and sincere thanks to our agent, Lisa Ekus, who helped shepherd all four books in this series from beginning to end, and to the team at Sterling Epicure for their guidance, hard work, and sincere dedication to making the project come to life, especially Carlo DeVito, Diane Abrams, Chris Thompson, and Blanca Olivieri.

ACKNOWLEDGMENTS FROM ANGELO GENTILE

Edible Twin Cities thanks, for starters, all of the local chefs, restaurateurs, caterers, farmers, artisans, cooks, food bloggers, cookbook authors, and others we reached out to for recipes—even a few who happened to be in places like Argentina and Korea when we called and who still came through for us. We were delighted to involve such an eclectic cross-section of local food lovers.

Next, we send a special shout-out to all of our supporters and advertisers of *Edible Twin Cities*, those area businesses and individuals who help keep our magazine going strong.

Thanks also to Michelle Hueser, former editor of *Edible Twin Cities*, who connected us to a variety of local and organic food devotees who submitted recipes.

We also express our thanks to *Edible Twin Cities* contributor Becky Poss, who capably assisted the book's photographer, Carole Topalian, when Carole visited the Twin Cities during a gloriously sunny week in early October. Becky also helped us contact a number of folks for recipes.

Additionally, we send a giant thanks to freelance writer Laura French, who also contributes to our magazine. Laura wrote two of the profiles that appear in the book, contacted a number of individuals for recipes, and then even submitted a few of her own.

We also offer great appreciation and admiration for Ann L. Burckhardt, who, like a wily relief pitcher coming in near the end of the game, helped us with recipe editing as we hit the late innings. Ann, who is now retired, was a writer and editor for the Taste section at the *Star Tribune* for twenty-four years.

Our gratitude also goes out to Beth Dooley. If Ann was our relief pitcher, Beth was our versatile utility player, adeptly fielding a number of positions for us. A longtime food journalist and cookbook author in Minneapolis, Beth wrote two of the profiles that appear in this book, submitted several of her recipes for the book, and, finally, assisted with recipe editing and headnote writing.

Special thanks also to Mark Weber, publisher of *Edible Twin Cities*, and general manager of Southwest Newspapers, the parent company of our magazine. Mark gave generously of his time to our cookbook project.

Finally, a personal note of thanks goes to Sally Peacock.

PROFILE CREDITS

Pages 6 and 80. Profiles: Danny Schwartzman, Common Roots Cafe and Catering, and Greg and Mary Reynolds, Riverbend Farm, were written by Laura French, a Minneapolis-based freelance writer who is a frequent contributor to *Edible Twin Cities.*

Pages 11 and 47. Profiles: Lucia Watson, Lucia's, and Jeanette Turner, a Minneapolis natural foods educator, were written by Sarah Tieck, a Burnsville-based freelance writer and a frequent contributor to *Edible Twin Cities.*

Page 40. Profile: Amy Lynn Brown and Heidi Andermack of Chowgirls Killer Catering was written by Amy Lyon, editor of the *Savage Pacer.*

Page 59. Profile: Sue Zelickson, food journalist and local food champion, was written by Melissa Gilman, former editor of *Savvy.mn.*

Pages 87 and 111. Profiles: Kristen Tombers, Clancey's Meats and Fish, and Lenny Russo, Heartland Restaurant & Farm Direct Market, were written by Beth Dooley, a Minneapolis food journalist whose latest book is *The Northern Heartland Kitchen.*

Page 123. Profile: Jack Gerten, St. Paul Farmers' Market, was written by Kristin Holtz, a writer and editor for Southwest Newspapers who also compiles the News & Trends section for *Edible Twin Cities.*

Page 131. Profile: Mark Ritchie, Minnesota Secretary of State, and founder of the Institute for Agriculture and Trade Policy, was written by Angelo Gentile, editor of *Edible Twin Cities.*

INDEX

A

Alcohol. *See* Drinks
Andermack, Heidi, 38, 40
Andrusko, Abby, 89
Appetizers or snacks, 31–53
  about: overview of, 31
  Buffalo (Bison) Steak Strips on a Bed of
    Greens, 36–37
  Chiles Stuffed with Feta, 48–49
  Chocolate Zucchini Bread, 35
  Cocktail Meatballs, Three Ways, 38–39
  Future Farm Basic Pesto, 33
  Iron Range Pasty, 32
  Marj's Cheese Ball, 42
  Mock Duck Banh Mi with Pickled Turnips
    and Carrots, 43
  Moist Date Nut Bread, 44
  Mom's Refrigerator Pickles, 44–45
  North Woods Frittata, 46
  Savory Zucchini Pancakes with Garlic
    Yogurt Herb Sauce, 41
  Tomatillo Dip, 50
  Truffled Kettle Corn, 52–53
  Two-Cheese Walnut Cream Pie, 34–35
  Wild Rice, Cashew, and Almond–Stuffed
    Mushrooms, 51
Apples
  about: Honeycrisp variety, 57
  Apple Cider Vinaigrette, 108
  Apple Cranberry Crumble Pie, 124–125
  Apple Crisp Parfaits with Caramel Sauce
    and Spiced Rum Whipped Cream, 126
  Apple Dressing, 65
  Apple Maple Syrup Sauce, 19
  Butternut Squash Soup with Honey-Thyme
    Honeycrisp Apples, 56–57
  Maple-Glazed Baked Apple, 132–133
  Sweet Porridge Apples, 16
  Wild Rice and Apple Salad, 82
Aztec Chile Hot Chocolate, 148

B

Banana bread, 24–25
Barley, in Pie Pumpkin-Barley Risotto,
  108–110
Barnstable, Hannah and Brady, 16
Basil, in Future Farm Basic Pesto, 33
Beans and legumes
  Black Bean Burgers, 102–103

Lemony Garlic White Beans, 70–71
Preserved Lemon Vegetable Tagine,
  116–117
Snowy Winter Lentil Stew, 112–113
Spring Pea Soup, 76–77
Beef
  Beef Braised in Coconut Milk, 86
  Beef Fajitas, 88–89
  Iron Range Pasty, 32
  Maple-Rhubarb Braised Beef, 100
  Salsa Verde Beef Stew, 90
Beets, in Farro Pilaf with Gold Beets, 66
Berries
  Apple Cranberry Crumble Pie, 124–125
  Blender Blueberry Soup, 129
  Blueberry-Lemon Oven Pancake, 20–21
  Blueberry Syrup, 22
  Cranberry Margaritas, 146–147
  Cranberry Orange Date Bread, 14
  Cranberry Pie, 130
  Curried Cranberries, 61
  Steamed Cranberry Pudding with Rum
    Sauce, 140
  Summer Fruit Fool, 134–135
  Sunday Morning Scones, 13
  Wild Rice Cranberry Soup, 83
Best Chocolate Pudding Ever, 138–139
Beverages. *See* Drinks
Billstein, Kelli, 112
Black Bean Burgers, 102–103
Blender Blueberry Soup, 129
Blueberries. *See* Berries
Blue Cheese and Apple Pork Chops, 92–93
Bonicelli, Laura, 3, 8, 19, 51, 77
Braatz, Jean, 25, 29, 58
Breads
  Chocolate Zucchini Bread, 35
  Corny Cornbread, 22
  Cranberry Orange Date Bread, 14
  Minnesota Farmer Banana Bread, 24–25
  Moist Date Nut Bread, 44
  Round Date Breads, 29
  Scandinavian Flatbread, 12
  Sunday Morning Scones, 13
  White Bread Sweet Rolls, 28
Breakfast dishes, 1–29
  about: overview of, 1
  Apple Maple Syrup Sauce, 19
  Blueberry-Lemon Oven Pancake, 20–21

Blueberry Syrup, 22
Butternut Squash Pancakes, 2–3
Corny Cornbread, 22
Cranberry Orange Date Bread, 14
Kids Cook Potato and Carrot Rösti Cakes,
  23
Lion's Tooth Eggs, 4–5
Minnesota Farmer Banana Bread, 24–25
Orange Yoghurt Pancakes, 26–27
Polenta Breakfast Pizza, 8
Pumpkin Pancakes, 7
Riverbend Farm Polenta, 9
Round Date Breads, 29
Scandinavian Flatbread, 12
Sunday Morning Scones, 13
Swedish Pancakes, 10
Sweet Corn Arepas with Red Pepper and
  Vegan Sausage, 15
Sweet Porridge Apples, 16
Turnip Rösti, 17
White Bread Sweet Rolls, 28
Breen, Jenny, 81
Brimley, The, 144
Broccoli, in Thai-Style Pasta, 114–115
Brown, Amy Lynn, 38, 40
Buffalo (Bison) Steak Strips on a Bed of Greens,
  36–37
Burckhardt, Ann L., 7, 74, 129, 136, 148
Butler, Carol J., 4, 124, 149
Butternut squash. *See* Squash

C

Cabbage
  Cabbage Soup, 58
  Coleslaw, 104
Carrots
  Ginger Ale–Glazed Carrots, 60
  Honey-Glazed Roasted Root Vegetables, 67
  Kids Cook Potato and Carrot Rösti Cakes,
    23
  Thai-Style Pasta, 114–115
Cauliflower, in Thai-Style Pasta, 114–115
Cheeses
  about: feta, 49
  Chiles Stuffed with Feta, 48–49
  Marj's Cheese Ball, 42
  Two-Cheese Walnut Cream Pie, 34–35
Cherne, Virginia, 137
Chicken

Chicken continued
    Grilled Country Chicken and Light
       Barbecue Marinade, 98–99
    Minnesota Harvest Salad with Chicken,
       106–108
Chiles Stuffed with Feta, 48–49
Chocolate
    Aztec Chile Hot Chocolate, 148
    The Best Chocolate Pudding Ever, 138–139
    Chocolate Zucchini Bread, 35
Chowgirls Killer Catering, 38, 40
Citrus
    Blueberry-Lemon Oven Pancake, 20–21
    Cranberry Orange Date Bread, 14
    Drink-sicle, 149
    Honey, Ginger, and Lemon Glaze, 38–39
    Iced Lemon Tea, 148
    Lemon-Ginger Pound Cake, 120–121
    Lemony Garlic White Beans, 70–71
    Orange Yoghurt Pancakes, 26–27
    Preserved Lemons, 116
Clancey's Meats and Fish, 87, 153
Cocktail Meatballs, Three Ways, 38–39
Coffee
    Coffee Toffee Bars with Almond Glaze, 127
    Midnight Garden Mocha, 142–143
Common Roots Cafe and Catering, 6, 7
Co-ops, 150–153
Corn. *See also* Polenta
    Corny Cornbread, 22
    Sweet Corn Arepas with Red Pepper and
       Vegan Sausage, 15
    Truffled Kettle Corn, 52–53
Country Pear Tart, 128
Cranberries. *See* Berries
CSA farms, 25, 80, 100, 131
Cucumbers
    Cucumber Melon Salad, 62–63
    Mom's Refrigerator Pickles, 44–45
Cuddy, Terry and John, 13
Cumbie, Patricia, 116
Curried Cranberries, 61

D

Dandelions, in Lion's Tooth Eggs, 4–5
Dates
    Moist Date Nut Bread, 44
    Round Date Breads, 29
Desserts
    about: overview of, 119
    Apple Cranberry Crumble Pie, 124–125
    Apple Crisp Parfaits with Caramel Sauce
       and Spiced Rum Whipped Cream, 126
    The Best Chocolate Pudding Ever, 138–139
    Blender Blueberry Soup, 129

Coffee Toffee Bars with Almond Glaze, 127
Country Pear Tart, 128
Cranberry Pie, 130
Lemon-Ginger Pound Cake, 120–121
Maple-Glazed Baked Apple, 132–133
Norwegian Fruit Soup, 136
Rhubarb Tart, 122
Rosemary/Maple Syrup, 141
Steamed Cranberry Pudding with Rum
    Sauce, 140
Summer Fruit Fool, 134–135
Wartime Cake, 137
Dooley, Beth, 20, 22, 55, 67, 72, 73, 82, 91,
    121, 132
Drinks
    about: sources for ingredients, 155–158
    Aztec Chile Hot Chocolate, 148
    The Brimley, 144
    Cranberry Margaritas, 146–147
    Drink-sicle, 149
    Iced Lemon Tea, 148
    Midnight Garden Mocha, 142–143
    The Recipe, 144
    Scotch Pie, 141

E

Early Fall Salad with Apple Dressing, 64–65
Edible Communities, Inc., vi
Eggplant, in Summer Gratin, 73
Eggs
    Lion's Tooth Eggs, 4–5
    North Woods Frittata, 46
    pancakes with. *See* Pancakes

F

Farmers, growers, markets, specialty shops,
    153–155
Farmers' markets, 150
Farro Pilaf with Gold Beets, 66
Ferndale Market, 61, 96, 103
Ferndale Turkey Meatloaf, 103
Fisher, Beth, 100
Fish Tacos with Mango Salsa and Coleslaw,
    104–105
Food co-ops, 150–153
French, Laura, 12, 144
French Meadow Bakery, 15
Fresh Tart blog, 26, 86
Frittata, 46
Fruit
    Norwegian Fruit Soup, 136
    Summer Fruit Fool, 134–135
Future Farm Basic Pesto, 33
Future Farm Food and Fuel, about, 33

G

Gabel, Jacqueline, 140, 147, 148
Garlic Yogurt Herb Sauce, 41
Gerten, Helen, 122
Gerten, Jack, 122, 123
Ginger
    Ginger Ale–Glazed Carrots, 60
    Honey, Ginger, and Lemon Glaze, 38–39
    Lemon-Ginger Pound Cake, 120–121
Good Life Catering, 81
Grass Fed Cattle Company, 89
Green beans, in Preserved Lemon Vegetable
    Tagine, 116–117
Grilled Country Chicken and Light Barbecue
    Marinade, 98–99

H

Harrison, Supenn, 115
Hazeltine National Golf Club, 107, 108
Heartland Restaurant, 109, 110, 111
History, edible, 7, 32, 43, 57, 82
Honey, Ginger, and Lemon Glaze, 38–39
Honey-Glazed Roasted Root Vegetables, 67

I

Iced Lemon Tea, 148
Iron Range Pasty, 32

K

Kate in the Kitchen blog. *See* Selner, Kate
Kids Cook, about, 23
Kids Cook Potato and Carrot Rösti Cakes, 23
Kiiskinen, Kathy, 32

L

Laab Moo and Khao Neow (Savory Chopped
    Pork Salad with Steamed Sticky Rice), 101
Lamb stew, 94–95
Linden Hill Meats, 87
Lion's Tooth Eggs, 4–5
Lucia's Restaurant, 10, 11, 41, 94

M

Mahi-Mahi Fish Tacos with Mango Salsa and
    Coleslaw, 104–105
Main dishes, 85–117
    about: overview of, 85
    Beef Braised in Coconut Milk, 86
    Beef Fajitas, 88–89
    Black Bean Burgers, 102–103
    Blue Cheese and Apple Pork Chops, 92–93
    Butternut Squash Lasagna, 97
    Ferndale Turkey Meatloaf, 103
    Grilled Country Chicken and Light
       Barbecue Marinade, 98–99

Laab Moo and Khao Neow (Savory Chopped Pork Salad with Steamed Sticky Rice), 101
Mahi-Mahi Fish Tacos with Mango Salsa and Coleslaw, 104–105
Maple-Rhubarb Braised Beef, 100
Midwinter Garlicky Lamb Stew, 94–95
Minnesota Harvest Salad with Chicken, 106–108
Pie Pumpkin-Barley Risotto, 108–110
Preserved Lemon Vegetable Tagine, 116–117
Roasted Pie Pumpkin, 110
Salsa Verde Beef Stew, 90
Savory Spicy Turkey Tenderloins, 96
Snowy Winter Lentil Stew, 112–113
Thai-Style Pasta, 114–115
Venison Loin in Pancetta with Cranberries, 91
Mango Salsa, 104
Maple-Glazed Baked Apple, 132–133
Maple Mustard Dressing—The Best Dressing Ever, 78
Maple-Rhubarb Braised Beef, 100
Marchan, Lupita, 50
Marj's Cheese Ball, 42
Meatballs, cocktail, 38–39
Meat sources, 87
Melon, in Cucumber Melon Salad, 62–63
Meyer, Stephanie A., 26, 86
Midnight Garden Mocha, 142–143
Midwinter Garlicky Lamb Stew, 94–95
Mills, Charli, 35
Minnesota Farmer Banana Bread, 24–25
Minnesota Farmers Union, 68
Minnesota-Grown Grilled Romaine Lettuce with Sea Salt, 68–69
Minnesota Harvest Salad with Chicken, 106–108
Mitchell, Paulette, 83, 104
Mock Duck Banh Mi with Pickled Turnips and Carrots, 43
Moist Date Nut Bread, 44
Mom's Refrigerator Pickles, 44–45
Montana, of River Rock Coffee, 143
Mushrooms, wild rice, cashew and almond-stuffed, 51
My Minnesota Farmer CSA, 25, 29

N
Nelson, Kat, 17, 43
North Woods Frittata, 46
Norton, James, 34
Norwegian Fruit Soup, 136
Nuts

about: benefits of walnuts, 65
Early Fall Salad with Apple Dressing, 64–65
Marj's Cheese Ball, 42
Moist Date Nut Bread, 44
Sweet Porridge Apples, 16
Two-Cheese Walnut Cream Pie, 34–35
Wild Rice, Cashew, and Almond–Stuffed Mushrooms, 51

O
Oats, in Sweet Porridge Apples, 16
Orange. See Citrus
Organizations, 158–159
Oskey, Dan, 140, 144

P
Pancakes
Blueberry-Lemon Oven Pancake, 20–21
Butternut Squash Pancakes, 2–3
Orange Yoghurt Pancakes, 26–27
Pumpkin Pancakes, 7
Savory Zucchini Pancakes with Garlic Yogurt Herb Sauce, 41
Swedish Pancakes, 10
Parisien, Barb, 44
Parsnips, in Honey-Glazed Roasted Root Vegetables, 67
Pasta
Butternut Squash Lasagna, 97
Thai-Style Pasta, 114–115
Pasty, Iron Range, 32
Patrin, Lisa, 126
Pears
Country Pear Tart, 128
Poached Pears, 72
Pea soup, 76–77
Peppers
Chiles Stuffed with Feta, 48–49
Preserved Lemon Vegetable Tagine, 116–117
Sweet Corn Arepas with Red Pepper and Vegan Sausage, 15
Pesto, 33
Peterson, Doug, 68
Peterson, Jane, 61, 96, 103
Pickles, refrigerator, 44–45
Picnic Operetta, 49
Pizza, breakfast, 8
Poached Pears, 72
Polenta
Polenta Breakfast Pizza, 8
Riverbend Farm Polenta, 9
Pork
about: nutritional value, 93

Blue Cheese and Apple Pork Chops, 92–93
Laab Moo and Khao Neow (Savory Chopped Pork Salad with Steamed Sticky Rice), 101
Warm Bacon and Spinach Salad with Maple Mustard Dressing—The Best Dressing Ever, 78–79
Poss, Becky, 60
Potatoes
Kids Cook Potato and Carrot Rösti Cakes, 23
Potato Gratin, 74–75
Preserved Lemon Vegetable Tagine, 116–117
Summer Gratin, 73
Preserved Lemon Vegetable Tagine, 116–117
Pumpkin
Pie Pumpkin-Barley Risotto, 108–110
Pumpkin Pancakes, 7
Roasted Pie Pumpkin, 110

Q
Quinoa salad, sweet and savory, 81

R
Raspberries. See Berries
Recipe, The, 144
Red Stag Supper Club, 52
Reiland, Jeanne, 99
Resources, 150–159
Reynolds, Greg and Mary, 6, 9, 80, 155
Rhubarb Tart, 122
Ries, Elizabeth, 97, 102, 138
Ritchie, Mark, 37, 130, 131, 150–152
Riverbend Farm, 6, 80, 155
Riverbend Farm Polenta, 9
River Rock Coffee, 143
Roasted Pie Pumpkin, 110
Root vegetables, honey-glazed roasted, 67
Rosemary/Maple Syrup, 141
Rösti, 17
Rösti cakes, 23
Round Date Breads, 29
Rum Sauce, 140. See also Spiced Rum Whipped Cream
Rush River Produce, 13
Russo, Lenny, 109, 110, 111
Rutabaga, in Honey-Glazed Roasted Root Vegetables, 67

S
Salads
Apple Cider Vinaigrette for, 108
Coleslaw, 104
Cucumber Melon Salad, 62–63

Early Fall Salad with Apple Dressing, 64–65
Laab Moo and Khao Neow (Savory Chopped Pork Salad with Steamed Sticky Rice), 101
Minnesota-Grown Grilled Romaine Lettuce with Sea Salt, 68–69
Minnesota Harvest Salad with Chicken, 106–108
Sweet and Savory Quinoa Salad, 81
Warm Bacon and Spinach Salad with Maple Mustard Dressing—The Best Dressing Ever, 78–79
Wild Rice and Apple Salad, 82
Salsa Verde Beef Stew, 90
Sandwiches. *See* Mock Duck Banh Mi with Pickled Turnips and Carrots
Sauces and dip
    Apple Cider Vinaigrette, 108
    Apple Dressing, 65
    Future Farm Basic Pesto, 33
    Garlic Yogurt Herb Sauce, 41
    Honey, Ginger, and Lemon Glaze, 38–39
    Mango Salsa, 104
    Maple Mustard Dressing—The Best Dressing Ever, 78
    Orchard Dressing, 81
    Swedish Meatball Gravy, 38–39
    Sweet Chili Sauce, 38–39
    Tomatillo Dip, 50
Sauces (sweet)
    Almond Glaze, 127
    Apple Maple Syrup Sauce, 19
    Blueberry Syrup, 22
    Rosemary/Maple Syrup, 141
    Rum Sauce, 140
    Spiced Rum Whipped Cream, 126
Sausage
    about: Clancey's, 87
    Sweet Corn Arepas with Red Pepper and Vegan Sausage, 15
Savory Spicy Turkey Tenderloins, 96
Savory Zucchini Pancakes with Garlic Yogurt Herb Sauce, 41
Sawatdee Thai Restaurant, 115
Scandinavian Flatbread, 12
Schneider, Nick, 49
Schwartzman, Danny, 6, 7
Scones, 13
Scotch Pie, 141
Selner, Kate, 14, 22, 44, 66, 71, 127
Seven Sundays Everyday Muesli, 16
Side dishes. *See also* Salads; Soups and stews
    about: overview of, 55
    Curried Cranberries, 61

Farro Pilaf with Gold Beets, 66
Ginger Ale–Glazed Carrots, 60
Honey-Glazed Roasted Root Vegetables, 67
Lemony Garlic White Beans, 70–71
Minnesota-Grown Grilled Romaine Lettuce with Sea Salt, 68–69
Poached Pears, 72
Potato Gratin, 74–75
Summer Gratin, 73
Simpson, Eric, 107, 108
Snowy Winter Lentil Stew, 112–113
Solo by Bonicelli. *See* Bonicelli, Laura
Soups and stews
    about: overview of, 55
    Butternut Squash Soup with Honey-Thyme Honeycrisp Apples, 56–57
    Cabbage Soup, 58
    Midwinter Garlicky Lamb Stew, 94–95
    Snowy Winter Lentil Stew, 112–113
    Spring Pea Soup, 76–77
    Wild Rice Cranberry Soup, 83
Southview Country Club, 57
Spiced Rum Whipped Cream, 126
Spring Pea Soup, 76–77
Squash
    Butternut Squash Lasagna, 97
    Butternut Squash Pancakes, 2–3
    Butternut Squash Soup with Honey-Thyme Honeycrisp Apples, 56–57
Steamed Cranberry Pudding with Rum Sauce, 140
Strip Club Meat & Fish Restaurant, 140, 144
Summer Fruit Fool, 134–135
Summer Gratin, 73
Sunday Morning Scones, 13
Swedish Pancakes, 10
Sweet and Savory Quinoa Salad, 81
Sweet Corn Arepas with Red Pepper and Vegan Sausage, 15
Sweet Porridge Apples, 16
Sweet potatoes, in Honey-Glazed Roasted Root Vegetables, 67

T
Tacos, fish, 104–105
Thai-Style Pasta, 114–115
Tomatillos
    about: using and storing, 90
    Tomatillo Dip, 50
Tombers, Kristin, 87
Trotter's Café, 128
Truffled Kettle Corn, 52–53
Turkey
    Early Fall Salad with Apple Dressing, 64–65
    Ferndale Turkey Meatloaf, 103

Savory Spicy Turkey Tenderloins, 96
Turner, Jennette, 46, 47, 62, 65, 78, 90, 93, 135
Turnips
    Honey-Glazed Roasted Root Vegetables, 67
    Mock Duck Banh Mi with Pickled Turnips and Carrots, 43
    Turnip Rösti, 17
Two-Cheese Walnut Cream Pie, 34–35

V
Vegan dishes
    Mock Duck Banh Mi with Pickled Turnips and Carrots, 43
    Preserved Lemon Vegetable Tagine (adaptation), 116–117
    Summer Gratin (adaptation), 73
    Sweet Corn Arepas with Red Pepper and Vegan Sausage, 15
Vegetables, in Preserved Lemon Vegetable Tagine (adaptation), 116–117. *See also specific vegetables*
Venison Loin in Pancetta with Cranberries, 91
Vlach, David, 57
Vrieze, Pam, 33

W
Warm Bacon and Spinach Salad with Maple Mustard Dressing—The Best Dressing Ever, 78–79
Wartime Cake, 137
Watson, Lucia, 10, 11, 41, 94
Weber, Mark, 42
White Bread Sweet Rolls, 28
Wild rice
    about: growing in Minnesota, 82
    Wild Rice and Apple Salad, 82
    Wild Rice, Cashew, and Almond–Stuffed Mushrooms, 51
    Wild Rice Cranberry Soup, 83
Wise Acre Eatery, 100
Woll, Kris, 28

Y
Yogurt
    Garlic Yogurt Herb Sauce, 41
    Orange Yoghurt Pancakes, 26–27

Z
Zelickson, Sue, 59
Zucchini
    Chocolate Zucchini Bread, 35
    Savory Zucchini Pancakes with Garlic Yogurt Herb Sauce, 41
    Summer Gratin, 73